ICONS

WEB DESIGN: MUSIC SITES

Ed. Julius Wiedemann

TASCHEN

HONGKONG KÖLN LONDON LOS ANGELES MADRID PARIS TOKYO

CONTENTS

CONTENTS

Music is everywhere. Now it's on the web.
Julius Wiedemann

For a long time our generation possessed music when we used to buy Vinyl, Cassettes and later on CDs. Before that we experienced music with radios, first AM and later on FM. And even before that, live performance was the only way to do it. But the truth is that sound is propagated in the air, and that's the way it reaches us. Music is just about reaching people, it does not matter if it is Jazz or Rock n' Roll, Pop or Dance, Reggae or Blues, Classic or Techno.

Music as we experience it today started to be shaped more than 100 years ago. The first prediction of radio waves was made in the 1860's by Scottish physicist James Clerk Maxwell. A bit later in 1866 the German physicist demonstrated the existence of radio waves. And finally in 1895 in Bologna, Italy, Guglielmo Marconi and brother Alfonso transmitted for the first time radio signals across a hill near their home.

Thomas Edison, who invented the first phonograph, for both recording and replaying sound, demonstrated the device for the first time on November 29, 1877. After that, there were a number of players that were mass-produced that helped popularize recorded music, such as the 45rpm record, and 78rpm record, culminating in a revolutionizing device and disc in 1948, invented by Hungarian born physicist Peter Carl Goldmark.

They were the 33 1/3 RPM disc and LP (long-playing) phonograph. This innovative system increased the playing time, and records were now produced with vinyl (polyvinyl chloride or PVC). Amazingly at that time, Goldmark also developed the "Highway Hi-Fi," which allowed drivers to play records in their cars, which initially were produced for Chrysler cars in 1956. This sounds quite mobile.

Some time before that, Radios were also starting to peak. Led by the invention of the vacuum tube diode by J. Ambrose Fleming in 1904 and the triode vacuum tube amplifier by Lee DeForest in 1906 the meaning of broadcasting as we know today starts to become reality, and first radio broadcasts are seen after 1909. Magnetic tape was first invented for recording sound by Fritz Pfleumer in 1928 in Germany, based on the invention of magnetic wire recording by Valdemar Poulsen in 1898.

The Compact Disc: a turning page in the digitalized music world. In the early 1970s, the compact disk was developed by Philips from its own 12 inch Philips Laservision disks. At the end of the 1970s, Philips, Sony, and other companies presented prototypes of digital audio discs. In 1979 Philips and Sony started to work together with the mission to design the new digital audio disc. Philips contributed the general manufacturing process, based on the video Laserdisc technology. Philips also contributed the Eight-to-Fourteen Modulation, EFM, which offers both a long playing time and a high resilience against disc handling damage such as scratches and fingerprints; while Sony contributed the error-correction method, CIRC. The Compact Disc reached the Asian market in 1982 and other markets the following year. (Billy Joel's 52nd Street was the first CD released commercially in Japan in October, 1982.)

The MP3 (MPEG-1 Audio Layer 3) conquers the world. It was invented and standardized in 1991 by a team of engineers directed by the Fraunhofer Society in Erlangen, Germany. On July 7, 1994 the Fraunhofer Society released the first software MP3 encoder called l3enc. With the first real-time software MP3 player Winplay3 (released September 9th, 1995) many people were able to encode and playback MP3 files on their PCs. Because of the relatively small hard drives back in that time (~500 MB) the technology was essential to store music for listening pleasure on a computer. After that there was just a boom of players, file sharing, portable MP3 players, etc. The release and popularization of the iPod device from Apple Inc. in the United States exemplifies the culmination of the technological perspectives. However, it was still difficult to buy music online, and users were basically relying on the conversion of the CDs into digital files to listen to "digital" music, as well as using (illegal) file sharing software.

As we have seen, the creation of systems seems to have always tried to strike more flexibility and mobility. So here we are with music also on the web. As the internet is also becoming more mobile and present in our daily lives, it give us the opportunity to experience music whenever we want. It can be a ring tone, or a complete track, or just samples of music you might want to buy, radio, music video-clips, etc.

Broadband has made life easier when dealing with music on the web. Good sites can instantly start playing music without any loading time, and can also have movie clips, photos and downloads available to visitors. Websites are now the main road to conquer new fans, and after conquering, establishing a relationship with them. The way we learn about music has changed. From radio to singles, there is a lot of reformulation in the formulas for artists and labels to achieve success. Today, more than ever in History, music is undergoing a big transformation. From production process, to the experience, and also how the whole industry works, have been changing at a fast pace.

I can still remember the first MP3 player I saw from Sony in the electronic Mecca called Akihabara in Japan, when still living there. After that there were almost monthly releases of different brands and devices that play digital music in the world. Going to Akihabara to see them started to become almost like sightseeing. The first models were really expensive and had comparatively a very small memory capacity. Today in Japan, most mobile phones play MP3, so they can have one device that integrates radio, MP3 Player, Digital TV, GPS, e-mails, Cash card and also telephone with all the agendas and calendars we know.

Moving to the book now, we have tried to give you cases and pages that serve as a reference for what has been developed so far, as well as giving you good ideas on how to experience music. There were a couple things that fascinated me and Daniel, my editor assistant, when editing the book. The amount of downloadable free (and legal) music is quite astonishing. There is also the fact that many sites play entire tracks continuously, so if you have internet, you can open that page in your browser and minimize the window, just to hear the music of your favourite artist or band, without actually having to buy it. Another thing is the quality of the sound. If you have good external speakers (not the ones from your computer, probably) you can enjoy music at its best. Quality has improved so much. There is also a huge amount of content to be enjoyed online, such as pictures, videos, blogs, shop, ring tones, goodies, etc.

What still seems to be going slowly is the usage of music in non-music sites. Slowly people will realize that a website can be like a film, that it can have a sound track. This can certainly enhance the appeal of the site and create an atmosphere that resonates the content.

We wish you all great enjoyment with the book.

the

La musique est partout. Maintenant sur la toile.

Julius Wiedemann

Longtemps, pour notre génération, posséder de la musique a signifié acheter des vinyles, des cassettes, puis plus tard des CD. Avant cela, il fallait écouter la radio, tout d'abord les grandes ondes, puis la FM. Et, avant encore, aller au concert, écouter la musique en direct. Mais à vrai dire, c'est dans l'air que le son se propage, et c'est par cette voie qu'il nous parvient. Or c'est justement ça, parvenir aux gens, que cherche la musique, peu importe qu'elle soit jazz ou rock n' roll, pop ou dance, reggae ou blues, classique ou techno.

La musique telle qu'on l'entend aujourd'hui a commencé à prendre forme il y a un peu plus de 100 ans. Le premier à émettre l'hypothèse des ondes radio, en 1860, fut le physicien écossais James Clerk Maxwell. Un peu plus tard, en 1866, le physicien allemand Hertz allait en démontrer l'existence. Et, finalement, en 1895, Guglielmo Marconi et son frère Alfonso transmettraient pour la première fois des signaux sonores au travers d'un fil, non loin de chez eux, à Bologne (Italie).

En 1877, Thomas Edison invente le premier phonographe, qui sert à la fois à graver et reproduire les sons, et, le 29 novembre de la même année, il fait la démonstration de son appareil pour la première fois. Viendront ensuite plusieurs supports de lecture qui, fabriqués en série, contribueront à populariser la musique enregistrée : le 78 tours, le 45 tours et, pour culminer la série, un appareil et un support révolutionnaires inventés en 1948 par le physicien d'origine hongroise Peter Carl Goldmark. Il s'agissait du disque tournant à 33 tours 1/3 par minute, et du phonographe LP (long-playing). Ce système novateur permettra d'accroître le temps d'écoute, et les disques seront désormais fabriqués en vinyle (polychlorure de vinyle ou PVC). Curieusement pour l'époque, Goldmark inventera également le "Highway Hi-Fi," dispositif censé permettre aux conducteurs de reproduire des disques dans leur voiture, et qui sera initialement fabriqué pour les modèles Chrysler en 1956. On le voit, ça commençait à bouger.

Les radios avaient fait leur apparition quelques temps auparavant. Annoncé par l'invention de la diode, ou tube à vide, par J. Ambrose Fleming en 1904, puis par celle de la lampe triode, dispositif amplificateur découvert par Lee DeForest en 1906, le phénomène de la radiodiffusion tel que nous le connaissons aujourd'hui devient alors réalité, et les premières émissions radiophoniques voient le jour à partir de 1909. La bande magnétique à enregistrer des sons sera quant à elle inventée par Fritz Pfleumer en 1928, en Allemagne, grâce à la création du premier enregistreur magnétique à fil d'acier par Valdemar Poulsen en 1898.

Le disque compact : un tournant dans l'histoire de la musique numérique. Au début des années 1970, Philips met au point le compact disque à partir de ses propres disques Laservision 12 inches. A la fin des années 1970, Philips, Sony et plusieurs autres sociétés présentent des prototypes de disques audio numériques. En 1979, Philips et Sony commencent à travailler ensemble avec pour objectif de concevoir le nouveau disque audio numérique. Philips y contribuera en développant le processus de fabrication, basé sur son expérience de la technologie du Laserdisc vidéo, ainsi que l'EFM (Eight-to-Fourteen Modulation), qui permet d'augmenter tout à la fois la capacité de stockage et la résistance du disque à la dégradation (rayures et traces de doigts) ; de son côté, Sony contribue à la méthode de correction d'erreurs, CIRC. Le compact disc atteint l'Asie en 1982, et les autres marchés dans les années qui suivent. ('52nd Street' de Billy Joël sera le premier CD commercialisé, au Japon, en octobre 1982.)

Le MP3 (MPEG-1 Audio Layer 3) conquiert le monde. Il a été inventé et standardisé en 1991 par une équipe d'ingénieurs dirigés par la Fraunhofer Society à Erlangen, Allemagne. Le 7 juillet 1994, Fraunhofer lance le premier logiciel de compression MP3, baptisé l3enc. Le premier logiciel de lecture en temps réel MP3 Winplay3 (lancé le 9 septembre 1995) permettra quant à lui à un nombreux public de coder et de reproduire des fichiers MP3 sur PC. Comme la capacité de mémoire des disques durs est encore relativement faible à l'époque (~500 MB), la technologie est essentielle pour stocker de la musique pour le plaisir. Un véritable boom de lecteurs, de partage de fichiers, de baladeurs MP3, etc. s'en suivra. Le lancement et la popularisation du lecteur portatif iPod par Apple Inc. aux États Unis illustrent parfaitement l'aboutissement des perspectives technologiques. Mais acheter de la musique online reste difficile et les utilisateurs sont obligés d'en passer par la conversion de CD en fichiers numériques pour écouter de la musique "numérique", et de recourir (illicitement) aux logiciels de partage de fichiers.

Comme on l'a vu, la création de systèmes semble avoir toujours aspiré à davantage de flexibilité et de mobilité. Désormais la musique est présente sur le Web. Et comme Internet gagne en mobilité et s'impose de plus en plus dans notre quotidien, il est désormais possible d'écouter de la musique n'importe où… Cela peut aller de la sonnerie de portable à la chanson complète, et du sampler à la radio, en passant par la musique de vidéoclips, etc.

Pour s'approvisionner en musique sur le Web, la bande large nous a facilité la vie. Sur les bons sites, on peut instantanément passer à l'écoute sans délai de chargement, ou visualiser des clips, des photos et des fichiers téléchargeables mis à la disposition des visiteurs. Les sites Web sont désormais la voie royale pour conquérir de nouveaux fans et, après la conquête, nouer des liens avec eux. La façon d'aborder la musique et de s'informer à son sujet a changé. De la radio aux CD simples, une foule de formules sont à la disposition des artistes et des labels pour réussir. Aujourd'hui, plus que jamais dans l'histoire, la musique est en train de vivre un bouleversement. De la production à l'écoute, en passant par le fonctionnement même de l'industrie, le panorama tout entier s'est brusquement transformé.

Je me souviens encore du premier lecteur MP3 que j'aie jamais vu, un Sony. C'était à Akihabara, la Mecque de l'électronique, au Japon où j'habitais encore. Après cela, pratiquement chaque mois, de nouvelles marques et de nouveaux reproducteurs de musique numérique ont été lancés dans le monde. Aller à Akihabara pour les voir commençait à devenir une excursion. Les premiers modèles étaient vraiment hors de prix et, comparés à ceux d'aujourd'hui, dotés d'une très faible capacité de mémoire. Aujourd'hui, au Japon, la plupart des téléphones portables sont équipés d'un lecteur MP3, et on peut donc avoir un seul et unique appareil avec radio, lecteur MP3 Player, TV numérique, GPS, e-mails, carte de crédit et téléphone, plus tous les agendas et autres calendriers que l'on connaît.

Pour en venir au livre, nous avons tâché d'y mettre des encadrés et des pages qui vous serviront de référence sur ce qui existe à ce jour, ainsi que de bonnes idées et des conseils d'écoute. Plusieurs choses nous ont surpris, Daniel, mon assistant, et moi-même, en publiant ce livre. La quantité de musique à télécharger gratuitement (et légalement) est absolument époustouflante. Le fait, également, que de nombreux sites reproduisent certains morceaux en continu, ce qui permet, lorsqu'on a Internet, d'ouvrir la page avec son navigateur, de minimiser la fenêtre, et d'écouter tranquillement son artiste ou son groupe préféré sans avoir à acheter la musique. Et puis aussi la qualité du son. Avec de bons haut-parleurs externes (autrement dit, pas ceux vendus avec l'ordinateur), on peut écouter de la musique dans les meilleures conditions. La qualité s'est énormément améliorée. Enfin, il existe une foule de contenus disponibles on-line : films, vidéos, blogs, boutiques, sonneries téléphoniques, promotions, etc.

Ce qui semble démarrer plus lentement, par contre, c'est la musique sur les sites non musicaux. Petit à petit, les gens réalisent qu'un site Internet peut, à l'instar d'un film, avoir sa propre bande-son. Une chose qui, à n'en pas douter, renforce le charme du site et crée une atmosphère qui en rehausse le contenu.

Très bonne lecture.

Musik ist überall. Und jetzt auch im Web.

Julius Wiedemann

Lange Zeit war für unsere Generation der Besitz von Musik nur möglich, wenn wir Langspielplatten, Musikkassetten oder später CDs kauften. Davor empfingen wir Musik durch das Radio, zunächst über AM und später über FM. Und noch früher war lediglich Live-Musik angesagt, und man musste sich schon zu der Musik hinbegeben. Tatsache ist jedoch, dass sich Klang nun einmal über die Luft verbreitet und uns auf diese Weise erreicht. Und Musik erreicht uns, egal ob es sich um Jazz oder Rock n' Roll, Pop oder Dance, Reggae oder Blues, Klassik oder Techno handelt.

Das Musikerlebnis, wie wir es heute kennen, begann seine Geschichte vor mehr als hundert Jahren. Radiowellen wurden 1860 erstmals von dem schottischen Physiker James Clerk Maxwell erwähnt. Ein wenig später, im Jahre 1866, wies der deutsche Physiker XXX die Existenz der Radiowellen nach. Und schließlich übertrugen 1895 in Bologna die Brüder Marconi und Alfonso Guglielmo zum ersten Mal Radiowellen über einen Hügel in der Nähe ihres Hauses.

Thomas Edison erfand 1877 den ersten Phonograph, der Klang sowohl aufzeichnen als auch wiedergeben konnte, und führte das Gerät erstmalig am 29. November jenes Jahres vor. Danach wurden eine Reihe von Geräten in Masse produziert, die aufgezeichnete Musik populär machten, wie zum Beispiel die 45rpm Platte und die 78rpm Platte. Der Physiker Peter Carl Goldmark, gebürtige Ungar, erfand schließlich 1948 ein revolutionierendes System, das aus einer 33 1/3 rpm Platte und einem LP-Phonograph bestand. Dieses bahnbrechende System erhöhte die Abspielzeit beträchtlich. Platten wurden nun aus Vinyl hergestellt (Polyvinylchlorid oder PVC). Erstaunlich für die damalige Zeit entwickelte Goldmark auch die "Highway HiFi"-Anlage, die Autofahrern das Abspielen von Platten in ihren Fahrzeugen ermöglichte. Diese Anlagen wurden 1956 zunächst für Autos der Firma Chrysler produziert und boten schon ziemlich viel Mobilität.

Ein wenig zuvor begann auch das Radio seinen Siegeszug. Durch die Erfindung der Röhrendiode durch J. Ambrose Fleming in 1904 und der Triode durch Lee DeForest in 1906 begann die Entwicklung des Runkfunks zu seiner heutigen Bedeutung. Die ersten Rundfunksendungen wurden ab 1909 ausgestrahlt. Auf Grundlage der Erfindung des Magnetondrahts von Valdemar Poulson in 1898 entwickelte Fritz Pfleumer 1928 in Deutschland das Magnettonband, das für Tonaufnahmen verwendet werden konnte.

Die Audio-CD revolutionierte die digitalisierte

Musikwelt. Die Firma Philips entwickelte in den frühen 70er Jahren die Compact Disk von ihren eigenen Philips Laservision-Disketten. Gegen Ende der 70er Jahre stellten Philips, Sony und andere Unternehmen ihre Prototypen digitaler Audo-CDs vor. 1979 begannen Philips und Sony eine Zusammenarbeit mit dem Ziel, die neue digitale Audio-CD zu entwickeln. Philips trug das auf der Video Laserdisc-Technologie basierende Herstellungsverfahren bei. Zudem brachte Philips die EFM-Modulation mit ein, die eine lange Spielzeit sowie eine hohe Widerstandsfähigkeit gegen Schäden bietet, die durch falsche Handhabung der CD enstehen können, wie zum Beispiel Kratzer oder Fingerabdrücke. Sony fügte das Fehlerkorrekturverfahren CIRC hinzu. Die Compact Disc erreichte Asien in 1982 und im Folgejahr weitere Märkte. ("52nd Street" von Billy Joel wurde 1982 in Japan als erste kommerzielle CD veröffentlicht.)

MP3 (MPEG-1 Audio Layer 3) erobert die Welt. Das Format MP3 wurde 1991 von einer Gruppe von Ingenieuren am deutschen Fraunhofer-Institut in Erlangen entwickelt und als Teil des MPEG-Standards festgeschrieben. Am 7. Juli 1994 stellte das Fraunhofer Institut den ersten MP3-Kodierer vor. Mit dem ersten Echtzeit-MP3-Player Winplay3 (veröffentlicht am 9. September 1995)

konnten viele Menschen auf ihren PCs MP3-Dateien kodieren und abspielen. Wegen der damaligen relativ kleinen Festplatten (~500 MB) war diese Technologie notwendig, um Musik für das Hörvergnügen duch den Computer zu speichern. Der nachfolgende Siegeszug von MP3-Kodierern und tragbaren MP3-Playern etc. gipfelte schließlich in der Entwicklung und Popularisierung des iPod Gerätes von Apple in den USA, was den technologischen Höhepunkt veranschaulichte. Es war jedoch immer noch schwierig, Musik online zu erwerben und die Anwender konnten "digitale" Musik nur hören, wenn sie CDs in digitale Dateien umwandelten oder (illegale) Software mit gemeinsamen Dateizugriff benutzten.

Wie wir gesehen haben, hat man bei der Entwicklung von Systemen immer versucht, noch mehr Flexibilität und Mobilität zu erreichen. Und nun gibt es sogar Musik im Web. Da auch das Internet in unserem Alltag immer mobiler und präsenter wird, eröffnet es uns die Möglichkeit, jederzeit und überall Musik zu erleben. Das kann ein Klingelton sein, ein ganzer Musiktitel oder Samples von Musik, die Sie vielleicht kaufen möchten, oder Radio, Musikvideoclips etc.

Die Breitband-Technologie hat den Umgang mit Musik aus dem Web einfacher gemacht. Gute

Websites können sofort und ohne vorherige Ladezeit Musik spielen, und stellen ihren Besuchern dabei auch noch Filmclips, Fotos und Downloads zur Verfügung. Websites stellen mittlerweile das Hauptmedium zur Eroberung neuer Fans dar und stellen eine Beziehung zu ihnen her. Die Erfahrung von Musik hat sich für uns verändert. Vom Radio zur Single - auf dem Weg zum Erfolg werden die Formeln für Künstler und Marken beträchtlich umgeschrieben. Mehr als jemals zuvor in der Geschichte unterliegt die Musik einer starken Wandlung. Die Produktion bis hin zum Erleben der Musik sowie das Funktionieren der gesamten Musikbranche ändern sich in immenser Geschwindigkeit.

Ich erinnere mich noch genau an den ersten MP3-Player von Sony, den ich bei Akihabara in Japan - dem Mekka für Elektronik - sah, als ich noch dort lebte. Später tauchten fast monatlich überall in der Welt neue Marken und Geräte auf, die digitale Musik spielten. Der Besuch bei Akihabara wurde zunehmend zu einer Besichtigungstour dieser Neuheiten. Die ersten Modelle waren sehr teuer und hatten eine vergleichsweise sehr kleine Speicherkapazität. Heute haben die meisten Mobiltelefone eine MP3-Funktion. Ein solches Gerät integriert Radio, MP3-Player, digitales Fernsehen, GPS, e-mails,

Cash Card und natürlich Telefon sowie alle bekannten Terminplanungs- und Kalender-Systeme.

In unserem Buch versuchen wir Beispiele und Sites anzuführen, die Ihnen als Hinweise und Vorschläge dienen werden, was bis jetzt entwickelt wurde und wie Sie Musik erleben können. Viele Dinge haben mich und meinen Lektor Daniel beim Editieren dieses Buches fasziniert. Die Menge an herunterladbarer, kostenfreier (und legaler) Musik ist ziemlich erstaunlich. Zudem spielen viele Websites kontinuierlich ganze Musikstücke. Wenn Sie also Internet haben, können Sie eine solche Website in Ihrem Browser öffnen, das Fenster minimieren und so einfach die Musik Ihres Lieblingsinterpreten oder Ihrer Lieblingsband hören, ohne dabei die Musik tatsächlich kaufen zu müssen. Eine andere Sache ist die Klangqualität. Falls Sie gute Lautsprecherboxen besitzen (wahrscheinlich nicht die von Ihrem Computer) können Sie Musik in ihrer besten Form genießen. Die Klangqualitäten haben sich enorm verbessert. Außerdem gibt es noch gewaltige Mengen weiterer interessanter Inhalte, auf die online zugegriffen werden kann, wie zum Beispiel Bilder, Videos, Tagebücher, Shops, Klingeltöne, Schnäppchen etc.

Die Verwendung von Musik auf nicht-
musikalischen Websites entwickelt sich nur
langsam. Die Betreiber erkennen jedoch
zunehmend, dass Websites wie ein Film sein und
auch einen Soundtrack haben können. Dies kann
mit Sicherheit die Attraktivität der Website
steigern und eine Atmosphäre schaffen, die den
Inhalt unterstützt.

Wir wünschen Ihnen viel Spaß mit unserem
Buch.

Madonna.com
Jon Sulkow (PROD4ever)

GETTING STARTED. When we were asked if we wanted to design Madonna's website, our collective mouths dropped open. We started blasting **Borderline** and jumping around the room. Finally, we snapped out of it and realized what a lot of work we had in front of us. I cannot tell you exactly how many hours this site took to produce. In fact, we are still making updates and adjustments to it. Suffice it to say, it was a huge amount of work - 6 people in our studio worked fulltime for 3 months, with many late nights, and are still working off and on to make it better + keep it fun.

We needed to start the project before any album artwork or even the album title was confirmed. We knew that the general theme had something to do with dancefloors and that the music was going to be a return to early club grooves for Madonna. The only thing we heard was about 20 seconds of the first single "Hung Up" over the telephone. Before we were allowed to listen, we had to swear that we were not taping on the other end. What we heard was the signature arpeggiated riff of the song -- it was undeniable dance. We began to think about what elements we could incorporate to express this dancefloor motif, while keeping the design broad enough to encompass all aspects of Madonna's

career as well as the new/unseen artwork.

Before we started, we asked ourselves "what do we want when we visit Madonna's site." As we poured through hundreds and hundreds of photographs people kept calling each other over to "Look at this one!" or that one. The emotional content of each photo was completely over-whelming, and we decided that if we visited the site WE wanted to see BIG Madonna photos.

We then set to work on comps. We spent weeks taking the site in all kinds of directions which ranged from maximalist collages to the minimalist layout that was finally chosen. I was visually inspired by a few modern Japanese design books I had. In these books I was seeing that a minimalist piece could still be vibrant and alive. Soft elements and hard elements could combine to make something electric + the use of color gradients was inspiring. We decided that it would be really cool if the entire website could be represented like a dancefloor grid, where all the elements in the site were like squares on a dancefloor that could be turned on and off. Each square would be a color gradient, simulating the glow of the dancefloor.

As we started to think about specific pages, we decided that we would have 2 main types of photo backgrounds in the site. The first would be

Madonna's raw untouched photos, which pack an emotional punch. The 2nd type would be photos highly screened with the color gradients. The colors would always have to be ethereal and electric. If any designer turned in a muddy or earthy gradient, it was immediately rejected.

INTERFACE. Originally, I wanted to create an interface where EVERY element of the site could be represented by a square on a grid which was ever present. I had even created a little flash interface so that all of the people working on the site with me could submit grid patterns + we could actually make the data jump and dance. Ultimately, this grand vision proved to be a very UNFRIENDLY interface, especially for an audience the size of Madonna's, so we scaled that back a bit.

There are remnants of my crazy grid all over the site. A good example is when you visit a specific album page, there is a little grid in the upper left which allows a quick jump to any other album page. As well, we kept as many of the buttons + data grids looking like dancefloor squares as possible + also tried to inject a little vintage drum machine button feel into the site's main navigation.

FUN WITH REQUIREMENTS. We were asked by Warner Brothers Records (WBR) that the main content of the site be built as AJAX/dhtml pages

and also that we build in at least one Flash 8 piece. We had never created a site with AJAX so it was very exciting for us to start researching it to see exactly what could be done. It also made us feel like we were very much in league with Madonna. She is known as an innovator who re-invents herself in sound and style with each album, and it was cool for us to think that we were helping her re-invent the web and innovate in that aspect of her career. Hopefully we were somewhat successful with this.

The AJAX/dhtml experiments led to many of the site's main features -- the most obvious being the desktop style - reloadable, draggable panels which can be minimized so that, again, you can look at big pictures of Madonna. Another was the BPM (Beats Per Minute) panel. WBR suggested to us that we do something with the concept of BPM. We came up with the idea of BPM represent-ing a user's mood. So a really high BPM = "I am bouncing off the walls, I am so happy I cant stand it" and a really low BPM = "I am mellow + I might look at clouds all day." It makes me happy that the user can have some fun little interactions with the site + I like the idea of the site being controlled (just a little) by the community.

For our flash 8 piece we designed a Madonna timeline which fluidly scrolls thru different aspects of Madonna's career in 3d. It makes use of flash 8's new bitmap filters to simulate depth of field in real time. Also -- each year is a square in a dancefloor grid + again we got to choose some great Madonna poses and looks to represent each year.

CREDITS:

- Art Direction and Design: Jon Sulkow (PROD4ever).
- Additional Design: Rob Adams (PROD4ever).
- Lead Programmer: Jon Luini (Chime).
- Additional Programming: Nick Hubben and Jordyn Bonds (PROD4ever).
- Executive Producer: Robin Bechtel (WBR).
- Project Management: Kathlene Kiernan (WBR), Robert Greenhood (G&C), Denise Furano (Semtex Girls) and Greg Brown (PROD4ever).
- Technical Director: Ethan Kaplan (WBR).
- There were also a ton of other people who were instrumental in making this project a success and we want to thank all of them for their support, especially, Will Claflin (PROD4ever), Jeff Watson (WBR) and Felix Turner.

Jon Sulkow likes Atari and monkeys. He lives in Boston Massachussets, where he founded the design company **PROD4ever** with people he met in bars and basements. In 1979, the pizza-powered company invented breakdancing. Now they spend most of their time doing graphics for artists + the entertainment industry. They are dedicated to making the web not boring and pushing their design skills. At least one of these claims is false. **<www.prod4ever.com>**

Madonna.com
Jon Sulkow (PROD4ever)

AU BOULOT. Lorsqu'on nous a demandé de concevoir le site Web de Madonna, nous sommes tous restés bouche bée. Un Borderline général a explosé et nous nous sommes mis à bondir de joie ça et là dans la pièce. Ce n'est qu'en redescendant de notre petit nuage que nous avons réalisé l'étendue du boulot qui nous attendait. Je ne saurais vous dire exactement combien d'heures nous avons consacrées à ce site. En fait, nous en sommes encore à l'actualiser et à le fignoler. Il suffira de dire que ça n'a pas été une mince affaire – 6 personnes du studio, à plein temps pendant trois mois, de nombreuses soirées à travailler très tard dans la nuit, et beaucoup d'énergie et de travail à y consacrer encore pour l'améliorer et qu'il reste attrayant.

Il a fallu entamer le projet sans maquette d'album, ni même la confirmation du titre de l'album. Nous savions juste que le thème général avait quelque chose à voir avec les dancefloors et que la musique serait en quelque sorte pour Madonna un retour aux ambiances disco. Le seul truc qu'on a pu entendre, et par téléphone en plus, c'est environ 20 secondes du premier single "Hung Up". Avant d'être autorisés à écouter, il a fallu qu'on jure que personne n'était en train d'enregistrer à l'autre bout du fil. Ce qu'on entendu, c'est le riff arpégé que reprend la

chanson – c'était indéniablement 'dance'. Là, on a commencé à se demander quels éléments incorporer pour exprimer ce motif disco, tout en gardant suffisamment d'ouverture pour rendre compte aussi bien des différentes facettes de la carrière de Madonna que de cette nouvelle et mystérieuse maquette.

Avant de commencer, on s'est demandé « Que cherche-t-on quand on visite le site Madonna ? ». Alors qu'on croulait sous des monceaux de photos, les gens n'arrêtaient pas de nous appeler pour nous proposer « Jette un œil à celle-ci ! » ou à cette autre. Le contenu émotionnel de chaque photo était vraiment stupéfiant... et on a donc décidé que, si nous visitions le site, NOUS voudrions voir de GRANDES photos de Madonna.

Après ça, on s'est attaqué aux compos. On a passé des semaines à balader le site dans toutes les directions, du collage maximaliste au montage minimaliste sur lequel nous avons finalement arrêté notre choix. Visuellement parlant, je me suis inspiré d'une poignée d'ouvrages de design japonais moderne que je possède. J'ai compris en les consultant qu'une pièce minimaliste peut aussi être vibrante et pleine de vie. On peut y associer des éléments légers et plus durs pour obtenir une certaine électricité ; et puiser l'inspiration dans les dégradés de couleur. On a décidé que ça serait pas mal de donner au site l'aspect d'une piste de dancefloor, chaque élément du site étant représenté sous la forme d'un carreau pouvant être allumé ou éteint. Chaque carreau aurait sa propre nuance de dégradé, de manière à simuler le scintillement d'une piste de disco.

Quand on a commencé à penser aux pages spécifiques, on a décidé de retenir 2 principaux types d'arrière-plans photographiques. Tout d'abord des clichés de Madonna non retouchés, pleins d'énergie émotionnelle. Mais aussi des photos très tramées dans les dégradés de couleur choisis. Des couleurs que nous avons voulu éthérées et électriques. Si quelqu'un se mettait à tomber dans les tons boueux ou terreux, sa proposition était immédiatement rejetée.

INTERFACE. À l'origine, je voulais créer une interface où CHAQUE élément du site serait représenté par un carreau, sur une sorte de grille qui était toujours présente. J'avais même mis au point une petite interface flash afin que les gens travaillant sur le site puissent me soumettre des modèles de grille ; et de nous permettre de faire littéralement bondir et danser les données. Finalement, cette grande idée s'est traduite par une interface extrêmement HOSTILE, surtout

pour une audience de la taille de celle de Madonna ; on l'a donc réduit quelque peu.

Il reste toutefois des lambeaux de mon immense grille un peu partout sur le site. En voici un exemple ; lorsqu'on consulte la page d'un album donné, il y a dans le coin gauche en haut de l'écran une petite grille qui permet de passer rapidement à une autre page d'album. De même, nous avons tâché de garder autant de boutons et d'éléments en forme de grille que possible ; et de donner à la page principale de navigation l'air d'une vieille boîte à rythmes.

FUN, MAIS AVEC DES EXIGENCES. Warner Brothers Records (WBR) nous a demandé de construire les contenus principaux du site sous forme de pages AJAX/dhtml, et aussi d'en faire au moins une au format Flash 8. Nous n'avions jamais créé de site avec AJAX, et c'est donc avec une certaine excitation que nous avons entrepris les recherches pour voir ce qui pouvait être fait exactement. Nous avions aussi le sentiment d'être tout à fait en phase avec Madonna. Elle est connue pour son esprit novateur et c'est quelqu'un qui ne cesse pas de se réinventer en termes de sonorité et de style, à chaque nouvel album ; c'était gratifiant pour nous de penser qu'à notre manière, nous contribuions à réinventer le Net, tout en innovant sur cet aspect de sa carrière. Heureusement, il semblerait que nous ayons réussi.

Les expériences avec AJAX/dhtml ont abouti à la création de la plupart des fonctions principales du site – la plus évidente étant le style de mise en page – des fenêtres rechargeables, déplaçables, qui peuvent être réduites, laissant ainsi place à de grandes photos de Madonna. Une autre était le panel BPM (Beats Per Minute). WBR nous a suggéré de faire quelque chose avec le concept de BPM. Nous avons envisagé l'idée d'un BPM représentant les réactions de l'utilisateur. Avec un BPM extrêmement élevé = "Je grimpe littéralement aux rideaux, je kiffe tellement que c'est trop" et un BPM ultra bas = "Je déprime grave + Je vais avoir le blues toute la journée." Ça me rend heureux de savoir que l'utilisateur peut s'amuser en interaction avec le site, et j'aime l'idée d'un site contrôlé (ne serait-ce qu'un tout petit peu) par la communauté.

Pour la pièce en Flash 8, nous avons conçu un plan de montage passant en revue différents aspects de la carrière de Madonna en 3d. Il fait usage des nouveaux filtres bitmap flash 8 pour simuler une profondeur de champ en temps réel. De plus –chaque année est représentée par un carreau de dancefloor ; là encore, nous avons choisi quelques-unes des postures et allures favorites de Madonna pour représenter chaque année.

CRÉDITS :

- Direction artistique et conceptuelle : Jon Sulkow (PROD4ever).
- Design additionnel : Rob Adams (PROD4ever).
- Programmeur principal : Jon Luini (Chime).
- Programmation additionnelle : Nick Hubben et Jordyn Bonds (PROD4ever).
- Producteur délégué : Robin Bechtel (WBR).
- Gestion du projet : Kathlene Kiernan (WBR), Robert Greenhood (G&C), Denise Furano (Semtex Girls) et Greg Brown (PROD4ever).
- Direction technique: Ethan Kaplan (WBR).
- Une foule de gens a par ailleurs contribué à la réussite de projet ; qu'ils soient tous remerciés de leur soutien, en particulier Will Claflin (PROD4ever), Jeff Watson (WBR) et Felix Turner.

Jon Sulkow aime Atari et les singes. Il vit à Boston, Massachusetts, où il a fondé la société de design **PROD4ever**, au gré de ses rencontres dans les bars et les sous-sols. En 1979, la 'pizza-powered company' a inventé le break dancing. Il consacre désormais le plus clair de son temps au design graphique, pour le compte d'artistes et de l'industrie du disque. Il s'emploie également à égayer le Web en y déployant ses talents de designer. Au moins une de ces affirmations est fausse. <www.prod4ever.com>

Madonna.com

Jon Sulkow (PROD4ever)

DER ANFANG. Als wir gefragt wurden, ob wir Madonna's Website gestalten möchten, fiel bei uns allen die Kinnlade herunter. Wir drehten Borderline auf maximale Lautstärke und hüpften im Büro umher. Schließlich regten wir uns ab und merkten, wieviel Arbeit uns bevorstand. Ich kann Ihnen nicht sagen, wieviel Stunden zur Erstellung dieser Website nötig waren. Eigentlich führen wir immer noch Updates und Anpassungen bei der Website durch. Es genügt aber zu sagen, dass es eine gewaltige Menge Arbeit war - 6 Mitarbeiter in unserem Studio arbeiteten für 3 Monate in Vollzeit, oft bis spät abends, und arbeiten immer noch ab und zu daran, um die Site zu verbessern und interessant zu halten.

Wir mussten mit der Arbeit anfangen, bevor die Vorlage des Albums oder sogar der Titel des Albums bestätigt wurden. Wir wussten nur, dass das generelle Thema etwas mit Dancefloor zu tun hatte und dass die Musik eine Rückkehr zu dem frühen Club-Groove von Madonna darstellen würde. Das einzige, was wir zu hören bekamen, waren ca. 20 Sekunden der ersten Single "Hung Up" über das Telefon. Bevor wir den Ausschnitt hören durften, mussten wir schwören, dass wir die Musik nicht am anderen Ende der Telefonleitung mitschnitten. Was wir hörten war das charakteristische Arpeggio-Riff des Songs -

und es war zweifellos Dance-Musik. Wir begannen darüber nachzudenken, mit welchen Elementen wir dieses Dancefloor-Leitmotiv darstellen könnten, während das Design der Website genug Platz bieten sollte, um alle Aspekte von Madonna's Karriere aufzunehmen sowie für die Darstellung des neuen, ungesehenen Albums.

Wir fragten uns zunächst: "Was wollen wir, wenn wir Madonna's Website besuchen?". Während wir uns durch Hunderte von Fotos durcharbeiteten hielten wir uns gegenseitig jedes einzelne unter die Nase mit Ausrufen wie "Schau dir das Foto mal an!", "Oder das...!". Der emotionale Inhalt jedes Fotos war absolut überwältigend und wir beschlossen, dass WIR auf der Website GROSSE Fotos von Madonna sehen wollten, wenn wir die Site besuchen würden.

Daraufhin fingen wir mit der Arbeit an. Wir verbrachten Wochen damit, die Website aus allen Blickwinkeln zu diskutieren, von großformatigen Collagen bis hin zu einem minimalistischen Layout, auf das wir uns schließlich auch einigten. Ich war visuell inspiriert durch einige moderne, japanische Designbücher, die ich besaß. In diesen Büchern sah ich, dass ein minimalistisches Stück immer noch dynamisch und lebhaft sein konnte. Weiche und harte Elemente können kombiniert werden, um etwas elektrisierendes zu schaffen und die Verwendung von Farbverläufen war beeindruckend. Wir entschieden, dass die Website ziemlich cool aussehen würde, wenn die gesamte Site als Dancefloor-Raster präsentiert wird, wo alle Elemente der Website wie Quadrate auf einer Tanzfläche dargestellt werden würden, die an- oder ausgeschaltet werden könnten. Jedes Quadrat würde einen Farbverlauf repräsentieren, der das Leuchten des Dancefloors simulierte.

Danach planten wir die einzelnen Seiten und beschlossen, zwei Haupttypen bei den fotografischen Hintergründen der Website zu verwenden. Der erste Typ würde aus den reinen, unberührten Fotos von Madonna bestehen, die sehr viel Emotionalität ausstrahlten. Der zweite Typ bestände aus Fotos mit hohen Farbverläufen. Die Farben sollten immer ätherisch und elektrisierend sein. Wenn ein Designer in einen schlammigen oder erdigen Farbverlauf verfiel, wurde das Design sofort abgelehnt.

DAS INTERFACE. Ursprünglich wollten wir ein Interface kreieren, bei dem JEDES Element der Website durch ein Quadrat auf dem immer präsenten Dancefloor-Raster dargestellt werden könnte. Ich hatte sogar ein kleines Flash-Interface entworfen, so dass alle Leute, die mit mir an der Website arbeiteten, ihre Raster

vorlegen konnten. Wir konnten die Daten sogar wirklich springen und tanzen lassen. Letztendlich entpuppte sich diese große Vision als ein sehr BENUTZERUNFREUNDLICHES Interface, besonders für die Größe eines Publikum wie Madonna's, und deshalb reduzierten wir es ein wenig.

Überall auf der Website gibt es Überbleibsel meines verrückten Rasters. Gute Beispiele sieht man, wenn man eine bestimmte Seite des Albums aufruft. Ein kleines Gitter in der linken oberen Ecke erlaubt einen schnellen Wechsel zu jeder anderen Seite des Albums. Wir behielten auch möglichst viele Schaltflächen und Datengitter, die wie Dancefloor-Quadrate aussehen, und versuchten zudem in die Hauptnavigation der Seite eine Schaltfläche für eine alte Drum-Maschine einzufügen.

SPASS AN DER HERAUSFORDERUNG. Wir wurden von Warner Brothers Records (WBR) gebeten, den Hauptinhalt der Website als AJAX/dhtml-Seiten zu konzipieren und mindestens einen Flash 8 einzubauen. Wir hatten noch nie zuvor eine Website mit AJAX entwickelt und fanden es deshalb recht spannend herauszufinden, was man genau damit anfangen konnte. Außerdem gab es uns das Gefühl, dass wir mit Madonna im Bunde sind. Sie ist als innovative Person bekannt, die sich bei jedem Album in Klang und Stil neu erfindet. Wir fanden es toll zu denken, dass wir ihr helfen würden, das Web neu zu erfinden und diesen Aspekt ihrer Karriere innovativ zu beeinflussen. Wir hoffen, dass wir damit erfolgreich waren.

Die AJAX/dhtml-Experimente führten zu vielen Hauptfunktionen der Website. Die offensichtlichste ist der Desktop-Stil - wiederladbare, verschiebbare Flächen, die minimiert werden können, so dass man auf große Bilder von Madonna blicken kann. Eine weitere Funktion war die BPM (Beats Per Minute)-Fläche. WBR schlug uns vor, etwas mit dem BPM-Konzept zu machen. Wir kamen auf die Idee, dass BPM die Stimmung des Besuchers wiedergeben könnte. Ein sehr hohes BPM = "Ich könnte in die Luft springen, ich bin so glücklich, dass ich es nicht mehr aushalten kann" und ein sehr niedriges BPM = "Ich bin entspannt, ich sehe mir den ganzen Tag die Wolken an". Es macht mich glücklich, dass der Anwender lustige kleine Interaktionen mit der Website haben kann und mir gefällt die Idee, dass die Site (ein wenig) von der Fangemeinde gesteuert wird.

Für unser Flash 8 entwarfen wir eine Madonna-Zeitleiste, die flüssig durch verschiedene Aspekte von Madonna's Karriere in 3D-Format scrollt. Die Funktion verwendet den neuen Bitmap-Filter von Flash 8, um Schärfentiefe in Echtzeit zu simulieren. Zudem wird jedes Jahr durch ein Quadrat in einem Dancefloor-Raster dargestellt und wir wählten dazu wieder ein paar der großartigen Madonna-Posen und -Anblicke.

NACHSPANN:
• Künstlerische Leitung und Design von Jon Sulkow (PROD4ever).
• Zusätzliches Design von Rob Adams (PROD4ever).
• Leitender Programmierer Jon Luini (Chime)
• Zusätzliche Programmierungen von Nick Hubben und Jordyn Bonds (PROD4ever).
• Produktionsleitung Robin Bechtel (WBR).
• Projektmanagement: Kathlene Kiernan (WBR), Robert Greenhood (G&C), Denise Furano (Semtex Girls) und Greg Brown (PROD4ever).
• Technische Leitung: Ethan Kaplan (WBR).
• Noch viele andere Personen haben dazu beigetragen, dass dieses Projekt zu einem Erfolg wurde und wir möchten ihnen allen für ihre Unterstützung danken, besonders Will Claflin (PROD4ever), Jeff Watson (WBR) und Felix Turner.

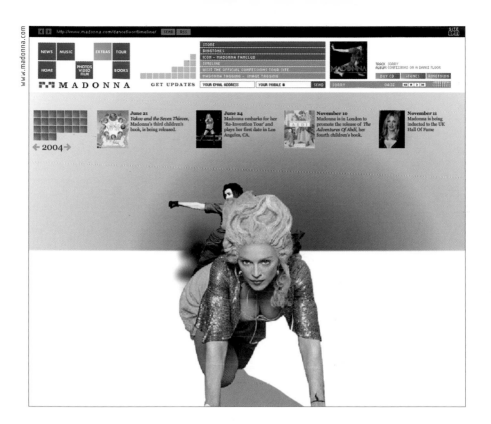

http://www.madonna.com/dancefloor/timeline/ SEND RSS

NEWS MUSIC EXTRAS TOUR
HOME PHOTOS BOOKS
VIDEO
FILM

MADONNA GET UPDATES YOUR EMAIL ADDRESS YOUR MOBILE # SEND SORRY 04:32

STORE
RINGTONES
ICON - MADONNA FANCLUB
TIMELINE
VISIT THE OFFICIAL CONFESSIONS TOUR SITE
MADONNA TAGGING - IMAGE TAGGING

TRACK SORRY
ALBUM CONFESSIONS ON A DANCE FLOOR
BUY CD iTUNES RINGTOWN

June 21
Yakov and the Seven Thieves, Madonna's third children's book, is being released.

June 24
Madonna embarks for her 'Re-Invention Tour' and plays her first date in Los Angeles, CA.

November 10
Madonna is in London to promote the release of *The Adventures Of Abdi,* her fourth children's book.

November 11
Madonna is being inducted to the UK Hall Of Fame

← 2004 →

Jon Sulkow mag Atari und Affen. Er lebt in Boston
Massachussets/USA, wo er das Design-Unternehmen
PROD4ever gründete, zusammen mit Leuten, denen er in Bars
und Kellerclubs begegnete. 1979 erfanden die pizza-
abhängigen Mitarbeiter des Unternehmens den Breakdance.
Heute verbringen sie die meiste Zeit damit, Graphiken für
Künstler und für die Unterhaltungsindustrie zu entwerfen. Sie
haben sich dazu verschrieben, das Internet nicht langweilig zu
gestalten und arbeiten permanent an ihren designerischen
Fähigkeiten. Mindestens eine dieser Behauptungen ist falsch.

SONY BMG Music UK
Daniel Ayers

Really, there shouldn't be a job for me at a record label. Or at least, not a specialist Digital Marketing position. I came through an interview 7 years ago despite requiring an explanation of the term 'mp3', and at the time 'New Media' was exactly that: building websites, marketing via e-mail, scanning everyone's baby photos for them- all new to the music industry.

Now, the internet, and the many and varied digital means of consuming music permeate almost every aspect of what a record label does. Understanding the online and digital possibilities for a record should not require more specialist knowledge than appreciating a half-page ad in Kerrang!.

I don't think that music itself has changed with the advent of the web; just as many great bands and just as many awful bands existed 15 years ago. Very few successful artists have been signed purely 'off the internet', or broken through from online activity alone; don't believe everything you read. It's been interesting to observe the boom-bust cycle caused by the perception of online/digital marketing within the industry. In 1999 we, along with anyone else with a website, were quoting figures in the millions (for almost any metric- users, impressions, mailing lists), and pretty much expecting that this direct access to consumers would translate into equally tasty sales. When that didn't quite happen, we dropped down the internal priority list somewhat, and we certainly haven't had any more 6-figure budgets to build sites with.

Right now it's boom again, and it's difficult to see another crash on the cards. Digital sales of songs, ringtones and video contribute enough to the charts and the business plan to make the area very much worthwhile. That doesn't mean, though, that online is a magical world, where wonderful consumers exist who will buy any old shit we throw at them (this is a common misconception, trust me). They are the same consumers who watch TV, listen to the radio and read the press. A great record is a great record, regardless of the format or the means of consumption.

What online does still give us, however, which no other media does, is a genuine direct contact with our consumers. Pre-online, you could argue a decent case for all marketing and promotion being aimed at high street retailers- consumers bought what was in the shops, so the label's job was to convince the retailers that they should stock more of our record than any other. Now, wonderfully, the consumer is liberated from that relationship. Virtual 'Racking', or 'Point Of Sale', are far, far less relevant at digital retail sites; as often as not, the user will arrive at the product directly via a link from another site, or an e-mail.

We know plenty of people who potentially want to buy our new records, because they've told us that they bought some of our old ones. We can e-mail them the links, and they can do just that. We just have to remember that 'can' doesn't mean 'will', unless we keep on producing good records and interesting communications. A proper communication strategy is absolutely vital to working a band over the course of a release. If we use our direct connection with the consumer purely to try and sell to them, they'll stop listening to us. If we make it interesting, exciting and entertaining then hell, people sometimes even look forward to getting e-mails/ SMS messages from us. And they definitely feel more inclined to buy the music when the time comes.

The other key aspect of this direct relation-ship, and one that much of the industry is still too removed from, is that the communication is (or should be) 2-way. Fans can very easily tell us what they think, of our music, our policies, our websites, anything. We'd be fools if we didn't listen. Label's are experts at protecting and exploiting the recording rights that they own. That doesn't (necessarily) mean we're peerless

when it comes to making records, and marketing and selling them. Obviously we like to think we're pretty good at it, but the internet has been fantastic at exposing hundreds and hundreds of people who have skills and ideas that we can clearly learn from. 'User-generated content' is the buzz-term for basically saying that 'people out there do cool shit'. We never fail to be amazed by the creativity and quality of the response when we run user-remix promotions, or invite fans to design alternate artwork for a release.

Building and running an artist website is always one of the most fun parts of a project. The sites I'm proudest of being involved in are <www.thecoopertempleclause.com> (for sheer weight of clever functionality), <www.kasabian. co.uk> (for truly helping to break the band when no radio station would touch them), <www. willyoung.co.uk> (because the flash stuff is so cool but the usability isn't compromised) and <www.lorrainemusic.co.uk> (ditto). And <www.columbia.co.uk>, which is my new favourite toy. News powered by RSS from the artist sites, totally easy to navigate and good looking. Go us.

Giving fans proximity to the artist through the official website is a process that has almost come full-circle. Of course we can have a blog on a site

from the band. It's very worthwhile, provided
they keep it up. That's not often a selling point in
itself any more though. Arguably, if you don't run
some sort of social-networking community
around your artist, you're off the pace. But just
doing the simple things well is enough to foster
and maintain a good relationship with the users,
and if they choose to spend their forum time
elsewhere, so be it. Artist sites aren't supposed
to be walled gardens; links are what glue the
internet together, and so long as these people
listen to us when we've got something to say, we
shouldn't be precious about what they do with the
rest of their time online.

The most exciting developing digital area for
me is wireless technology. When mp3 players/
mobile phones are routinely wireless, and
services exist to buy tracks over that connection,
the direct relationship will reach its ultimate
worth. Not that I'm looking forward to designing
more sites for a 200x200px screen res, though...

DESIRE Designed by Star/Ruler London, UK, 17.06.06 13:15:38

LORRAINE   VIEW BUILD HELP

NEWS   GALLERY   LIVE   MAILING   RELEASES   LORRAINE   COMMUNITY   FORUM   MOBILE   STORE

NEWS   RSS

23/05/06 WAP me - How many times have you been sat on
a bus, or a train, or a park bench, or... [ok, enough], and
thought: "If only I could check when and where Lorraine are
next playing. I have to have another fix of their music".

Very often, undoubtedly.

Luck, and technology, are now on your side, since you can
point your phone's WAP browser at **wap.lorrainemusic.co.uk**
and get all the key info from this site on your mobile (just a
bit smaller).

The WAP site also carries all the relevant news stories from
the website (except this one, which wouldn't make sense), and
of course is your portal to Lorraine ringtones and wallpapers as
well.

If you click the WAP link above on your computer browser, you
will get a bunch of instructions on different ways to access the
site.

NEWS ARCHIVE

WAP me

**Transatlantic Flight coming
July 17th**

New shows a-plenty

Feel It in at 29

Single reviews round-up

Feel It released/ new photos

Feel It out Monday 10th

New site mastheads

Page 1 of 3 **NEXT >>**

FEATURED ITEM

LISTEN TO TRANSATLANTIC FLIGHT MIXES

LORRAINE
Transatlantic flight

3:25

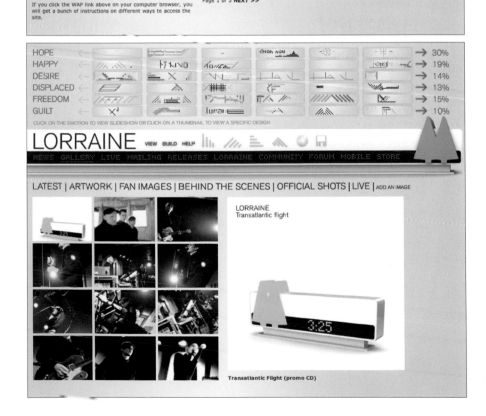

HOPE ← → 30%
HAPPY ← → 19%
DESIRE ← → 14%
DISPLACED ← → 13%
FREEDOM ← → 15%
GUILT ← → 10%

CLICK ON THE EMOTION TO VIEW SLIDESHOW OR CLICK ON A THUMBNAIL TO VIEW A SPECIFIC DESIGN

LORRAINE   VIEW BUILD HELP

NEWS   GALLERY   LIVE   MAILING   RELEASES   LORRAINE   COMMUNITY   FORUM   MOBILE   STORE

LATEST | ARTWORK | FAN IMAGES | BEHIND THE SCENES | OFFICIAL SHOTS | LIVE | ADD AN IMAGE

LORRAINE
Transatlantic flight

3:25

Transatlantic Flight (promo CD)

SONY BMG Music UK
Daniel Ayers

En fait, je ne devrais pas bosser pour un label discographique. Ou tout au moins, pas comme spécialiste du marketing numérique. Il y a sept ans de cela, je me suis assez bien tiré d'un entretien, bien qu'il ait fallu m'expliquer le sens de 'mp3', or à l'époque, chez 'New Media', le boulot c'était justement ça : construction de sites Web, marketing via courrier électronique, scannage des photos des gosses de tout le monde... autrement dit tout ce qu'il y avait de plus nouveau dans l'industrie de la musique.

Maintenant, Internet et les moyens numériques nombreux et variés de consommer de la musique imprègnent quasiment tous les aspects du travail d'une compagnie discographique. Comprendre les possibilités on-line et numériques qui s'offrent à un enregistrement ne devrait pas demander plus savoir spécialisé que de se rendre compte qu'une pub d'une demie page dans Kerrang! sera probablement vue par des fans de rock.

Je ne crois pas que la musique elle-même ait changé avec l'avènement du Net ; il y avait tout autant de bons groupes, et de mauvais, il y a 15 ans que maintenant. Très peu d'artistes à succès ont été pris sous contrat purement 'off the internet', ou ont percé uniquement grâce à leur activité on-line ; il ne faut pas croire tout ce qu'on

lit. Il est intéressant d'observer la perception en dents de scie dont fait l'objet le marketing on-line/numérique au sein de l'industrie. En 1999, comme tout propriétaire de site Web, nous tablions sur des chiffres millionnaires (pour la plupart des métriques utilisées, impressions, mailing lists), et nous espérions bien que cet accès direct aux consommateurs se traduirait par des ventes également juteuses. Comme cela ne s'est pas produit, il a fallu en rabattre sur la liste de priorités internes, et c'en a été fini des budgets de construction de site à 6 chiffres.

Voilà maintenant que ça repart de plus belle, et on voit mal comment pourrait se produire un nouveau crash. La vente numérique de chansons, de sonneries de portables et de vidéo contribue à soutenir les ventes, et le business plan à rentabiliser le secteur. Mais ça ne fait pas de 'on-line' un mot magique, ni de la toile un endroit où de merveilleux consommateurs sont prêts à acheter n'importe quelle merde qu'on leur balance (erreur assez communément répandue, croyez-moi). Ce sont les mêmes consommateurs que ceux qui regardent la télé, écoutent la radio et lisent la presse. Un bon disque est un bon disque, quels qu'en soient le format ou les moyens de consommation.

Ce que la vente en ligne nous apporte en

revanche, contrairement à d'autres médias, c'est un vrai contact direct avec nos consommateurs. Avant elle, on pouvait argumenter pas mal, car, comme toutes les ventes et promotions étaient destinées au commerce de détail, les consommateurs achetaient ce qu'il y avait en magasin, et le boulot du label consistait à convaincre les détaillants d'avoir en stock son produit plutôt qu'un autre. Aujourd'hui, et c'est heureux, le consommateur s'est libéré de ce rapport contraignant. Le 'rayonnage' ou le 'Point de vente' virtuel a nettement moins d'importance sur les sites de vente numérique au détail ; le plus souvent, l'utilisateur arrive au produit directement via un lien trouvé sur un autre site, ou par l'intermédiaire d'une adresse électronique. La plupart des acheteurs potentiels de nos nouveaux disques ont déjà acheté auparavant certains de nos produits plus anciens, et ils nous le disent. Nous pouvons leur envoyer des liens par mail, et ils n'ont plus qu'à s'en servir. Encore faut-il qu'ils le veuillent, et que nous continuions à produire de bons disques et des communications intéressantes. Une stratégie de communication appropriée est absolument vitale pour qu'un groupe fonctionne le temps d'un lancement. Si nous n'utilisons notre connexion directe avec le consommateur que pour essayer de vendre, il

cessera de nous écouter. Quand nous parvenons à la rendre intéressante, séduisante et divertissante, il arrive même que les gens attendent avec impatience nos courriels et nos messages SMS. Et, le moment venu, ils sont d'autant plus désireux et pressés d'acheter.

Autre aspect clé de cette relation directe, aspect dont l'industrie ne tient d'ailleurs pas suffisamment compte : la communication est (ou devrait être) à double sens. Les fans peuvent très facilement nous dire ce qu'ils pensent, de notre musique, de nos politiques, de nos sites... de tout. Nous serions fous de ne pas les écouter. Les labels sont devenus de vrais experts en matière de protection et d'exploitation des droits d'enregistrement qu'ils détiennent. Ça ne veut pas nécessairement dire que nous sommes les meilleurs quand il s'agit de fabriquer des disques, de les promouvoir et de les vendre. Evidemment, on aime bien penser qu'on est très bons, mais Internet a été un moyen fantastique de faire émerger des centaines et centaines de gens talentueux et pleins d'idées dont nous devons absolument nous inspirer. 'Contenu généré par l'utilisateur' est le terme de jargon généralement employé pour dire simplement qu'il y a là 'des gens qui font des trucs très sympas'. On ne manque jamais d'être surpris par la créativité et la qualité de la réponse quand on lance des promos user-remix, ou quand on invite les fans à concevoir une maquette alternative pour un lancement.

Construire et gérer le site Web d'un artiste est toujours l'une des meilleures parties d'un projet. Les sites auxquels je suis fier d'avoir participé sont <**www.thecoopertempleclause.com**> (pour son ingéniosité de fonctionnement remarquable), <**www.kasabian.co.uk**> (pour avoir réussi à faire connaître le groupe alors qu'aucune radio n'en parlait), <**www.willyoung.co.uk**> (parce que les trucs en Flash sont géniaux, sans en compromettre le fonctionnement pratique) et <**www.lorrainemusic.co.uk**> (idem). Et <**www. columbia.co.uk**>, mon nouveau jouet favori : des news gérées par RSS à partir des sites d'artistes, le tout vraiment beau à regarder et de navigation facile. Allez-y voir.

Si on fait tomber les barrières entre fans et artistes par le biais d'un site officiel, la boucle est presque bouclée. Bien sûr, on peut avoir un blog sur le site d'un groupe. C'est très utile, à condition qu'ils le gardent. En soi, ce n'est plus un point de vente. Disons-le, si on ne tisse pas une espèce de socialité en réseau autour de l'artiste, on est à côté de la plaque. Mais il suffit de bien faire les choses les plus simples pour nourrir et entretenir de bonnes relations avec les utilisateurs ; et s'ils décident d'aller passer ailleurs leur temps de forum, c'est leur droit. Les sites d'artistes ne sont pas des chasses gardées ; les liens assurent la cohésion de l'Internet, et du moment que les gens écoutent ce que vous avez à dire, il n'y a pas à se préoccuper de ce qu'ils font du reste de leur temps on-line.

Pour moi, la technologie sans fil est le domaine de création numérique le plus excitant. Quand les lecteurs mp3 et les portables sans fil seront plus courants, et qu'il existera des services pour acheter des 'tracks' par ce biais-là, la relation directe aura atteint son apogée. Ce qui ne veut pas dire que je me voie en train de concevoir davantage de sites en définition 200x200px ...

www.kasabian.co.uk

HOME
RELEASES
GALLERY
SHOP
MOVEMENT
SPEAK

LATEST NEWS   RSS

MARLAY PARK, DUBLIN
03.Apr 2006.

Kasabian have announced a show ahead of their
V2006 headline appearance, in Dublin.

The band will play Marlay Park with Faithless on
August 17th.

Tickets go on-sale on April 10th, via
www.ticketmaster.ie or on a 24hr credit card line.
+353 1 4569 569.

CONFIRMED FOR ROCK IN RIO
23.Mar 2006.

Kasabian have been confirmed on the line-up for
this year's Rock In Rio festival in Lisbon, Portugal.

The festival runs from June 2nd-4th, and Kasabian
play on the 3rd.

More info about the event at rockinrio-lisboa.sapo.pt

V2006 HEADLINE SLOT
27.Feb 2006.

It has just been confirmed that the band will headline
the second stage at this summer's V Festival.

On Saturday August 19th, Kasabian will be at the
Chelmsford Hylands Park site, moving to Stafford
Weston Park the following day (August 20th).

Tickets for the festival go onsale at 9am this Friday
(March 3rd), and you'll be able to find full details at
www.vfestival.com

Kasabian first played the V Festival in 2004, when
they opened the stage that they're now headlining.

NOTICE

LIVE FROM BRIXTON ACADEMY

KASABIAN

MAILING LIST

Enter mobile # to   E-mail Address:
receive Kasabian
texts (optional):

Date of Birth:
| Day ▼ | Month ▼ | Year ▼ |

Location:
--- Select Country --- ▼

By signing up you will receive mails about
Kasabian and possibly similar acts on their
label. To make sure your info isn't sold to
any other 3rd parties, leave this box ticked. ☑

Join

Home / Releases / Gallery / Shop / Movement / Speak   © 2006 Kasabian // Columbia Records // Kleber Design

---

SONY BMG Music UK
Daniel Ayers

Ich sollte wirklich nicht bei einer Plattenfirma arbeiten. Oder wenigstens nicht als Experte für Digital-Marketing. Vor sieben Jahren landete ich in diesem Job durch ein Bewerbungsgespräch, obwohl man mir den Ausdruck 'MP3' erklären musste, und zu jener Zeit ging es bei den 'Neuen Medien' um folgendes: Konzipieren von Websites, Marketing durch e-mails, Einscannen von jedermanns Baby-Fotos - all dies war ganz neu für die Musikindustrie.

Nun ist es das Internet, und die vielen unterschiedlichen digitalen Möglichkeiten des Musikkonsums durchdringen fast alle Aktivitäten, die eine Plattenfirma betreffen. Die Online- und digitalen Möglichkeiten für die Musikindustrie sollten einfach zu verstehen sein, genau wie man weiss, dass eine halbseitige Werbung in Kerrang! wahrscheinlich von Leuten gesehen wird, die Rock mögen.

Ich denke nicht, dass sich die Musik seit Beginn des Webs verändert hat; es gibt so viele großartige Bands und so viele schlechte Bands wie vor 15 Jahren. Nur wenige erfolgreiche Künstler sind 'direkt aus dem Internet' unter Vertrag genommen worden oder hatten ihren Durchbruch nur durch Online-Aktivitäten; glauben Sie nicht alles was Sie lesen. Es ist interessant gewesen, die Auf- und Abschwünge

der Sichtweise des Online/Digital-Marketings innerhalb der Musikindustrie mitzuverfolgen. So wie alle anderen mit einer Website kalkulierten wir in 1999 noch Zahlen in Millionenhöhe (für alles mögliche - Anwender, Auflagen, Mailing-Listen), und waren uns ziemlich sicher, dass dieser direkte Zugang zu den Konsumenten zu satten Umsätzen führen würde. Als dies nicht so ganz eintraf, mussten wir unsere interne Prioritäten anders setzen und hatten mit Sicherheit kein sechsstelliges Budgets mehr, um Websites zu konzipieren.

Jetzt boomt die Branche wieder und ein erneuter Absturz ist nicht abzusehen. Der digitale Verkauf von Songs, Klingeltönen und Videos trägt genug zu den Charts und den Geschäftsplänen bei und das Geschäft lohnt sich sehr. Das heißt aber nicht, dass der Online-Markt eine Zauberwelt ist, in der es wundervolle Käufer gibt, die jeden alten Dreck kaufen, den wir ihnen anbieten (das ist eine verbreitete falsche Vorstellung, glauben Sie mir). Es handelt sich um die gleichen Konsumenten, die fernsehen, Radio hören und Zeitung lesen. Eine gute Platte ist eine gute Platte, egal welches Format oder welche Mittel des Konsums bestehen.

Das was uns das Online-Marketing bringt, und was kein anderes Medium schafft, ist ein wirklich unmittelbarer Kontakt zu unseren Kunden. Zuvor konnte man sagen, dass eine ordentliche Werbung und gutes Marketing auf die Einzelhändler an der Haupteinkaufsstraße abzielen mussten. Die Konsumenten kauften das, was es in den Geschäften gab. Deshalb war es Aufgabe der Plattenfirma, die Geschäftsinhaber davon zu überzeugen, sich mehr mit ihren Platten einzudecken, als mit denen von anderen. Heute ist der Konsument auf wunderbare Weise von dieser Einschränkung befreit. Die eigentlichen 'Lager' oder die 'Verkaufsstellen' sind bei digitalen Verkaufs-Websites viel weniger relevant; oft stößt der Anwender auf das Produkt direkt über den Link einer anderen Website oder über e-mail. Wir kennen genug Leute, die vielleicht unsere neuen Platten kaufen wollen, da sie uns gesagt haben, dass sie einige unserer alten Platten gekauft hatten. Wir können diesen Leuten die Links per e-mail zusenden und sie können dann genau das tun. Wir müssen nur daran denken, dass 'können' nicht automatisch 'werden' heißt, es sei denn, wir produzieren weiterhin gute Platten und bieten interessante Kommunikation an. Eine gute Kommunikationsstrategie ist unerlässlich, um eine neue Band bis zur Veröffentlichung zu bringen. Falls wir unsere direkte Verbindung zu

den Konsumenten nur benutzen, um unsere Produkte zu verkaufen, dann hören sie uns nicht mehr zu. Wenn wir die Veröffentlichung aber sehr interessant, spannend und unterhaltsam ankündigen, freuen sich die Leute sogar manchmal richtig auf unsere e-mails und SMS-Nachrichten. Und wenn es soweit ist, fühlen sie sich in jedem Fall eher geneigt, die neue Musik auch zu kaufen.

Ein weiterer Hauptgesichtspunkt dieser unmittelbaren Beziehung zum Konsumenten, und davon ist ein großer Teil der Branche immer noch zu weit entfernt, ist dass die Kommunikation von beiden Seiten ausgeht (oder ausgehen sollte). Fans können uns sehr einfach mitteilen, was sie über uns denken - über unsere Musik, unsere Vorgehensweise, unsere Website - einfach alles. Wir wären sehr dumm, wenn wir ihnen nicht zuhören würden. Plattenfirmen sind Experten darin, ihre Aufnahmerechte zu schützen und zu verwerten. Das bedeutet nicht (unbedingt), dass wir unvergleichlich gut Platten machen und vermarkten können. Natürlich denken wir, dass wir ganz darin gut sind, doch das Internet ist phantastisch dafür geeignet, uns in Kontakt mit aberhundert Menschen kommen zu lassen, die gute Fähigkeiten und Ideen haben, von denen wir wirklich lernen können. 'Verbrauchererzeugter

Inhalt' ist das Schlagwort dafür, dass Leute da draussen ziemlich gute Sachen machen. Wir staunen immer wieder über die Kreativität und Qualität der Beiträge, wenn wir unsere Kunden-Remix Promotionen durchführen oder Fans dazu einladen, künstlerische Beiträge zu einer Veröffentlichung zu senden.

Das Konzipieren und die Betreuung der Website eines Künstlers ist immer ein Projektbereich, der am meisten Spaß macht. Die Websites, bei denen ich sehr stolz bin, mitgewirkt zu haben, sind <www.thecoopertempleclause. com> (wegen der raffinierten Funktionalität), <www.kasabian.co.uk> (weil wir der Band zum Durchbruch verhelfen konnten, als kein Radiosender sie haben wollte), <www.willyoung. co.uk> (da die Flash-Funktion so cool, doch die Bedienbarkeit nicht beeinträchtigt ist) und <www.lorrainemusic.co.uk> (dito). Und <www. columbia.co.uk>, mein neues Lieblingsspielzeug. Die Nachrichten werden von den Künstlerseiten durch RSS zur Verfügung gestellt, total einfach zu bedienen und sehen gut aus. Schauen Sie es sich einmal an.

Durch die offiziele Website können Fans Nähe zu den Künstlern aufbauen, und dieser Prozess ist fast zu einem geschlossenen Kreislauf geworden. Wir können natürlich ein Blog auf einer

Seite der Band haben, denn das ist äußerst lohnenswert, vorausgesetzt, er bleibt dort. Das sollte allerdings nicht das einzige Verkaufsargument sein. Wenn man um den Künstler herum nicht eine Art soziales Netzwerk für die Fangemeinde schafft, kann man wohl nicht mehr Schritt halten. Durch ein paar einfache und schöne Dinge kann man eine gute Beziehung zu den Anwendern pflegen und halten, und wenn diese ihre Forumzeit woanders verbringen möchten, dann ist es eben so. Künstler-Websites sind keine ummauerten Gärten und Links halten das Internet zusammen. Solange die Leute zuhören, wenn wir ihnen etwas zu sagen haben, sollten wir sie mit dem Rest ihrer Zeit online machen lassen, was sie wollen.

Die spannendste Entwicklung des digitalen Bereiches ist für mich die drahtlose Technologie. Wenn MP3-Player / Mobiltelefone alle standardmäßig drahtlos funktionieren und Service-Anbieter existieren, die Musiktitel über diese Verbindung anbieten, wird die direkte Ansprache des Konsumenten ihr Maximum erreichen. Nicht dass ich mich darauf freue, mehr Sites für eine Bildschirmauflösung von 200x200 Pixel zu kreieren, doch....

THE COOPER TEMPLE CLAUSE

MAKEPOVERTYHISTORY.ORG

FORTHCOMING GIGS

24/05/06 - Bierkeller, Bristol, United Kingdom
Tickets: 01179 299 008 // www.seetickets.com
Venue info: www.bierkeller.co.uk

25/05/06 - Kings College, London, United Kingdom
Tickets: 020 7848 1588 // www.seetickets.com
Venue Info: www.kclsu.org

26/05/06 - Academy 2, Birmingham, United Kingdom
Tickets: SOLD OUT

27/05/06 - Rock City, Nottingham, United Kingdom
Tickets: 0115 941 2544 // www.seetickets.com

29/05/06 - King Tuts, Glasgow, United Kingdom
Tickets: SOLD OUT

30/05/06 - 53 Degrees, Preston, United Kingdom
Tickets: 01772 894 861 // www.seetickets.com
Venue info: www.53degrees.net

31/05/06 - Academy 2, Manchester, United Kingdom
Tickets: 0161 832 1111 // www.ticketline.co.uk

02/06/06 - Cockpit, Leeds, United Kingdom
Tickets: SOLD OUT

03/06/06 - Empire, Middlesbrough, United Kingdom
Tickets: 01642 247 755 // www.seetickets.com

04/06/06 - Underground, Stoke, United Kingdom
Tickets: 01782 206 000 // www.seetickets.com

05/06/06 - Wedgewood Rooms, Portsmouth, United Kingdom
Tickets: 02392 863 911 // www.seetickets.com

GIGS IN BRIEF

24/05/06 - Bristol
- - - - - - - - - - - - - - - - - - -
25/05/06 - London
- - - - - - - - - - - - - - - - - - -
26/05/06 - Birmingham
- - - - - - - - - - - - - - - - - - -
27/05/06 - Nottingham
- - - - - - - - - - - - - - - - - - -
29/05/06 - Glasgow
- - - - - - - - - - - - - - - - - - -
30/05/06 - Preston
- - - - - - - - - - - - - - - - - - -
31/05/06 - Manchester
- - - - - - - - - - - - - - - - - - -
02/06/06 - Leeds
- - - - - - - - - - - - - - - - - - -
03/06/06 - Middlesbrough
- - - - - - - - - - - - - - - - - - -
04/06/06 - Stoke
- - - - - - - - - - - - - - - - - - -
05/06/06 - Portsmouth
- - - - - - - - - - - - - - - - - - -

GIG ARCHIVE

Press, fan reviews & images

FEATURED SECTION

Interactive Music Sites
Craig Swann (CRASH!MEDIA)

Music has the incredible ability to link both time and space through memory. How many of us can hear a song and instantly be transported to a specific moment in our lives? Music creates emotion and it is this emotion that acts as a bond to memory. As a communication tool, music is extremely effective in this ability to affect emotion and feelings. It is this unique capacity that sound possesses that has kept me interested in not only working with sound, as a powerful medium, but as an interactive element that can be driven by the user.

Audio is too often an overlooked element in online and interactive development. With the invention of Looplabs, my main purpose was to use audio in an engaging way which allowed the audio to not be a passive element, but something which was controlled, directed and created by the user. This was a new concept at the time, and to this day is still something that I believe is under utilized.

The actual creation of Looplabs.com began as nothing more than a personal experiment, but quickly grew into becoming the most widely used and experienced music mixing application on the Internet. When Flash 5 was released it came with a new set of controls to manipulate sound in real time. With these new tools, new ways of

interacting with sound became possible.

When thinking about, or working with, sound as an interactive component it requires a different approach and methodology. Generally the concept of sound is linear and holistic, however when working in interactive audio it is essential to look at it from a sub-level. How do the different elements and pieces of audio work together to create a soundscape. Rhythm, melody and tempo. The interplay of these elements as they are modified and controlled shift the feeling generated by the music. It is an interesting and rewarding experience when working directly with this interchange and to be enveloped in the process of creation.

From the thousands of emails that have been written in response to these interactive music sites, the one thing that has been the most rewarding has been the knowledge of knowing that they have changed the way that many people think about music. For many people music is something that is only experienced second-hand. Without the skills or knowledge to play an instrument people have been resolved to enjoy it simply through listening and not creating. By developing these interactive tools, people from all walks of life have been welcomed into the world of sound creation. From children to seniors,

I have received emails filled with thanks for opening their eyes (and ears) to the joy that is making music. Technology and interactivity have allowed music to be created in ways that before were not possible. No longer do we need to perform music via instruments. We can remix, manipulate, direct and control it through nothing more than clicks of the mouse.

Since the birth of Looplabs I have had the pleasure of developing interactive music sites and applications for some of the world's largest brands. Working with clients such as Bacardi, Miller Brewing, Calvin Klein and Sony we have continually pushed the envelope of interactive music making. Music mixers, sequencers, samplers and remixers have been developed to allow for different interactive experiences.

With the Bacardi Freestyle project this was taken a step further to allow for the integration of more than just music, but the addition of vocals. Users could remix and create the music track, but also have the ability to add their own vocals on top of this in real time. It was the first time online users could rap or sing through a simple web interface and create songs that were truly unique to them.

The concept of interactive audio has also led to looking at new ways of defining the gaming experience. Working on a project with Sony for the new PSP portable gaming device we developed an application that took game customization to a whole new level. Through a flash based online application users could select tracks from the WipeOut Pure game and remix the audio tracks that came with it. Using simple yet powerful tools users could seamlessly remix these songs to make them completely their own. The novel aspect of the project was that after remixing a track it could be downloaded directly to the PSP device. Once downloaded the users could select their newly created remix as the background music for the game as they played. This is the start of a whole new direction in integrating interactive audio into experiences that go beyond just the web.

However, interactive audio doesn't always just mean the ability to remix music in the traditional sense. The same technology can be used to redefine the concept of music making for online experiences. Several other applications have been built for the creation of generative audio. This means using the computer to write and arrange the music. Code becomes the conductor. By creating a library of sounds, and simple code constructs, we are able to generate music that is never the same. For instance the background music for a site can be generated so that it is never the same. Each unique user hears a unique interpretation of the music. Like hearing a band perform music live, it is always slightly different, slightly improvised. These abilities now exist, and are the areas that I am now exploring.

Music is one of the most powerful and expressive mediums in our lives and as technology advances it allows us to express sound in new and exciting ways. The future of interactive audio is an exciting one, and one that I hope begins to bring us all closer together and in harmony.

Craig Swann is founder and Chief Imagination Officer of the award-winning interactive design agency **CRASH!MEDIA**. Craig has been working in the online world since 1995 and has been a core part of the Flash® community since its inception. As an educator, curator, speaker, and writer of new media technologies, Craig has given 20 international talks on Flash, written and contributed to seven Flash books, and curated over a dozen new media events featuring some of the world's brightest Flash and interactive developers. His Flash work at CRASH! has received over a dozen awards and has been featured in both print and on television. Craig's interactive audio work has developed into the multi-award winning online music application Looplabs, which has been used by such clients as Coca-Cola, Miller, Bacardi, Calvin Klein, Toyota, Sony, and others. **<www.crashmedia.com>**

Interactive Music Sites
Craig Swann (CRASH!MEDIA)

La musique a l'incroyable faculté de relier le temps et l'espace au travers de la mémoire. Combien d'entre nous ne peuvent-ils pas, en effet, entendre une chanson sans être instantanément ramenés en pensée à un moment particulier de leur vie ? La musique crée l'émotion et c'est l'émotion qui fait le pont avec la mémoire. En tant qu'outil de communication, la musique est extrêmement efficace, justement à cause de cette aptitude à susciter émotion et sentiments. C'est cette capacité unique qui m'a amené à m'intéresser au travail sur le son, non seulement en tant que moyen puissant, mais aussi comme élément pouvant être dirigé par l'utilisateur.

En matière de création on-line et interactive, l'aspect audio est trop souvent négligé. En inventant Looplabs, mon principal objectif était de l'utiliser d'une manière séduisante qui lui permettrait de ne plus être un élément passif, mais quelque chose que l'utilisateur puisse contrôler, diriger et créer. C'était un nouveau concept à l'époque, et je crois qu'il reste sous-utilisé.

Simple expérience personnelle au départ, l'actuelle création de Looplabs.com s'est rapidement imposée comme l'application Internet de mixage musical la plus largement utilisée et écoutée. Lorsque le lecteur Flash 5 a été lancé, il comprenait une nouvelle série de contrôles permettant de manipuler le son en temps réel. Avec ces nouveaux outils, de nouvelles voies pour interagir avec le son se sont ouvertes.

Penser le son, ou le travailler comme un composant interactif requiert une approche et une méthodologie différentes. En général, on conçoit le son de manière linéaire et holistique, alors qu'en audio interactive il est essentiel de le considérer à un niveau inférieur. Comment les différents éléments et les différentes pièces du travail audio s'assemblent-ils pour créer un paysage sonore ? Le rythme, la mélodie et le tempo. L'interaction de ces éléments, à mesure qu'on les modifie et qu'on les contrôle, transforme le sentiment suscité par la musique. C'est une expérience passionnante et valorisante que de travailler directement sur cet échange et de se plonger dans le processus de création.

À la lecture des milliers de courriers électroniques reçus au sujet de ces sites de musique interactive, la chose la plus gratifiante aura été de se rendre compte qu'ils avaient changé, chez pas mal de gens, la façon de percevoir la musique. Pour beaucoup, la musique reste quelque chose dont on ne fait pas l'expérience par soi-même. Faute d'aptitude, ou faute de connaissances suffisantes pour jouer d'un instrument, la plupart se contente d'écouter la musique et se résigne à ne pas créer. Grâce à ces outils interactifs, des gens de tous bords ont désormais accès au monde de la création sonore. J'ai reçu des tas de courriels, émanant d'enfants comme de personnes âgées, pour me remercier de leur avoir ouvert les yeux (et les oreilles) à la joie de faire de la musique. La technologie et l'interactivité ont dégagé des voies de création musicale impraticables jusqu'ici. Les instruments ne sont plus indispensables : on peut remixer, manipuler, diriger et contrôler la musique, il suffit pour cela de quelques clicks de souris.

Depuis la naissance de Looplabs, j'ai eu le plaisir de développer des sites et des applications de musique interactive pour quelques-unes des plus grandes marques du monde. Travailler avec des clients tels que Bacardi, Miller Brewing, Calvin Klein et Sony, nous a conduit à pousser le bouchon de plus en plus loin dans la matière. Des mélangeurs, des séquenceurs, des samplers et des remixeurs ont été mis au point pour permettre diverses expériences interactives.

Avec le projet Bacardi Freestyle, une étape supplémentaire a été franchie pour faciliter l'intégration d'un élément supplémentaire : les voix. Les utilisateurs ont ainsi pu remixer et créer une plage musicale en rajoutant leur propre voix en surimpression et en temps réel. Pour la première fois, ils ont pu rapper ou chanter on-line grâce à un simple interface Web, et créer des chansons vraiment uniques pour eux-mêmes.

Le concept d'audio interactif a également conduit à chercher de nouvelles voies de définition du jeu. Dans le cadre d'un projet avec Sony pour la nouvelle console de jeux portable PSP, nous avons mis au point une application permettant de personnaliser le jeu d'une manière entièrement neuve. Au travers d'une application flash on-line, les utilisateurs pouvaient sélectionner des morceaux dans WipeOut Pure game et en remixer les pistes audio. A l'aide d'outils simples mais puissants, ils avaient la possibilité, en continu, de remixer ces chansons et de les transformer à leur guise. L'aspect novateur du projet tenait au fait qu'une fois remixée, la musique pouvait être directement téléchargée dans la console PSP, permettant ainsi aux utilisateurs de sélectionner leur nouveau remix et de l'écouter en fond sonore tout en jouant. Une direction entièrement nouvelle venait d'être prise en intégrant l'audio interactive dans des expériences allant au-delà du web.

Cependant, l'audio interactive ne signifie pas toujours possibilité de remixer de la musique au sens traditionnel. La même technologie peut être employée pour redéfinir le concept de composition musicale en termes d'expériences on-line. Plusieurs autres applications ont été mises au point pour créer de l'audio générative. En utilisant par conséquent l'ordinateur pour composer et écrire les arrangements. Le code devient alors le chef d'orchestre. En se constituant une bibliothèque de sons et de simples unités de construction codées, on peut créer de la musique qui ne cesse de changer. Par exemple, le fond sonore d'un site peut être conçu de telle manière qu'il se modifie sans arrêt. Chaque utilisateur en entend une interprétation unique. Comme à l'écoute d'un groupe en live, la musique est toujours différente, légèrement improvisée. Toutes ces possibilités existent désormais et ce sont les domaines que j'explore en ce moment.

La musique est l'un des moyens d'expression les plus forts qu'il nous soit donné d'expérimenter, et la technologie, à mesure qu'elle progresse, nous permet d'explorer par les sons de nouvelles et passionnantes voies. Vu l'avenir prometteur de l'audio interactif, j'espère qu'elle nous amènera bientôt à nous rapprocher les uns des autres et à vivre en harmonie.

Craig Swann est le fondateur et le "Chief Imagination Officer" de l'agence de design interactif plusieurs fois primée CRASH!MEDIA. Craig œuvre sur la toile depuis 1995 et il est partie prenante de la communauté Flash® depuis sa création. En tant qu'éducateur, conservateur, conférencier et écrivain en matière de nouvelles technologies de l'information, Craig a donné une vingtaine de communications internationales au sujet de Flash, il a écrit et contribué à sept livres sur Flash et organisé une douzaine d'événements sur la nouvelle communication avec la participation des plus grands créateurs mondiaux de la conception graphique et interactive en Flash. Le travail qu'il a mené en la matière pour CRASH! lui a valu une douzaine de récompenses et a été diffusé aussi bien dans la presse qu'à la télévision. Le travail audio interactif de Craig s'est traduit par LoopLabs, application de musique on-line plusieurs fois primée, qui a été utilisée par des clients tels que Coca-Cola, Miller, Bacardi, Calvin Klein, Toyota, Sony, entre autres. <www.crashmedia.com>

Interactive Music Sites
Craig Swann (CRASH!MEDIA)

Musik hat die wunderbare Fähigkeit, in unserer Erinnerung Zeiten und Orte miteinander zu verbinden. Wie oft hören wir einen Song und werden dadurch augenblicklich in eine bestimmte Zeit unseres Lebens versetzt? Musik erweckt Emotionen und es sind diese Emotionen, die eine Verbindung zu unserem Gedächtnis herstellen. Als extrem effektives Kommunikationswerkzeug kann Musik Emotionen und Gefühle beeinflussen. Diese einzigartige Kapazität der Töne hat mein Interesse daran erhalten, mit Ton nicht nur als wirkungsvolles Medium, sondern auch als interaktives Element zu arbeiten, das von dem Anwender gesteuert werden kann.

Das Audio-Element wird in der Online- und Interaktiv-Entwicklung zu häufig übersehen. Mit der Erfindung von Looplabs wollte ich die Audio-Technik aktiv benutzen und aus ihrer passiven Rolle befreien. Audio ist etwas, das durch den Anwender gestaltet, kontrolliert und gesteuert werden kann. Dies war zur damaligen Zeit ein völlig neues Konzept und ist meines Erachtens immer noch ein Element, das nicht häufig genug genutzt wird.

Looplabs.com begann eigentlich mit nichts anderem als einem persönlichen Experiment, doch es entwickelte sich schnell zu der am meisten benutzten und erfahrensten Anwendung

für Musikbearbeitung im Internet. Mit Flash 5 kam schließlich ein neues Set von Bedienelementen heraus, mit dem Töne in Echtzeit manipuliert werden konnten. Mit diesen Werkzeugen wurden neue Wege des Interagierens mit Ton möglich.

Die Denkweise über oder Arbeit mit Tönen als interaktive Komponente erfordert einen unterschiedlichen Ansatz und andere Methoden. Im Allgemeinen ist das Konzept von Ton linear und ganzheitlich, doch wenn man in der interaktiven Audiotechnik arbeitet, sollte man Ton von einer anderen Ebene aus betrachten. Wie wirken die verschiedenen Elemente und Bereiche der Audio-Arbeit zusammen, um eine Geräuschkulisse zu schaffen? Rhythmus, Melodie und Geschwindigkeit. Das Zusammenspiel dieser modifizier- und steuerbaren Elemente verändert die Gefühle, die durch die Musik hervorgerufen werden. Es ist eine interessante und lohnende Erfahrung, direkt mit diesem Wechselspiel zu arbeiten und in dem Schaffungsprozess eingebunden zu sein.

Tausende von e-mails sind als Reaktion auf diese interaktiven Musik-Sites geschrieben worden. Das Schönste daran ist zu wissen, dass sie bei vielen Menschen das Denken über Musik verändert haben. Für viele Menschen ist Musik etwas, was sie nur aus zweiter Hand erleben können. Ohne Fähigkeiten oder Kenntnisse zum Spielen eines Instruments beschränken sie sich darauf, Musik einfach nur zu konsumieren und nicht selbst zu erzeugen. Durch die Entwicklung dieser interaktiven Werkzeuge können Menschen aus allen Gesellschaftsschichten die Welt der Tonschöpfung betreten. Ich habe e-mails von Kindern bis zu Senioren erhalten, die voller Dank dafür waren, dass ihnen die Augen (und Ohren) für die Freude am Musikmachen geöffnet wurden. Durch Technologie und Interaktivität kann nun Musik auf eine Art und Weise geschaffen werden, die vorher nicht möglich war. Wir müssen nicht länger Instrumente spielen, um Musik zu machen. Wir können Musik neu abmischen, manipulieren, leiten und steuern, und das nur durch ein paar Mausklicke.

Seit der Geburt von Looplabs hatte ich das Vergnügen, interaktive Musik-Sites und Anwendungen für einige der weltgrößten Marken zu entwickeln. Durch die Arbeit mit Kunden wie Bacardi, Miller Brewing, Calvin Klein und Sony konnten wir kontinuierlich die Entwicklung von interaktiver Musik steigern. Musik-Mixer, Sequencer, Sampler und Remixer wurden entwickelt, um unterschiedliche interaktive Musikerlebnisse zu ermöglichen.

Bei dem Bacardi Freestyle-Projekt wurde noch ein Schritt weitergegangen und die Möglichkeit geschaffen, zusätzlich zu Musikelementen auch noch Stimmen zu integrieren. Anwender konnten nun das Musikstück nicht nur selbst kreieren und neu abmischen, sondern in Echtzeit auch ihre eigene Stimme hinzufügen. Online-Anwender konnten so erstmalig durch ein einfaches Web-Interface rappen oder singen und Songs schaffen, die für sie einzigartig sind.

Das Konzept der interaktiven Audio-Technik hat auch dazu geführt, neue Wege bei Spielsoftware zu suchen. In einem Projekt mit Sony für das neue tragbare PSP-Spielgerät entwickelten wir eine Anwendung, die eine neue Ebene der Spielanpassung erreichte. Mit einer auf Flash basierenden Online-Anwendung konnte man Musiktitel aus dem Spiel WipeOut Pure auswählen und die mitgelieferten Audiotitel remixen. Durch einfache, aber leistungsfähige Funktionen konnte der Anwender diese Songs nahtlos neu abmischen und sie so individuell gestalten. Der neuartige Aspekt des Projektes bestand darin, dass man einen Titel nach dem Remix direkt auf das PSP-Gerät herunterladen konnte. Nach dem Download konnte der Anwender sein neu geschaffenes Remix als Hintergrundmusik während des Spiels wählen. Dies ist der Anfang einer ganz neuen Richtung bei der Integration von interaktiver

Audiotechnik in Bereiche, die über das Internet hinausgehen.

Interaktive Audiotechnik bedeutet jedoch nicht immer nur die Möglichkeit, Musik im herkömmlichen Sinne neu abzumischen. Die gleiche Technologie kann benutzt werden, um das Konzept des Schaffens von Musik online neu zu definieren. Etliche weitere Anwendungen wurden für die Erzeugung generativer Audiotechnologie entwickelt. Mit ihrer Hilfe kann über den Computer Musik geschrieben und arrangiert werden. Ein Code wird zum Dirigenten. Durch das Schaffen von Ton-Bibliotheken und einfacher Code-Konstruktionen sind wir in der Lage, Musik zu kreieren, die niemals gleich ist. Zum Beispiel kann die Hintergrundmusik für eine Website so erzeugt werden, dass sie immer anders ist. Jeder einzelne Besucher der Website hört eine einzigartige Interpretation der Musik. So wie bei den Live-Auftritten einer Band ist die Musik immer ein wenig anders und ein bisschen improvisiert. Diese Möglichkeiten bestehen nun und auf diese Gebiete konzentrieren sich meine aktuellen Forschungen.

Musik ist eines der kraftvollsten und ausdrucksstärksten Medien unserer Zeit und der Fortschritt der Technologie ermöglicht uns, Töne auf neue und aufregende Art wiederzugeben. Die Zukunft der interaktiven Audiotechnologie ist spannend und ich hoffe, dass sie uns alle in Harmonie näher zusammenbringt.

Craig Swann ist Gründer und Generaldirektor der preisgekrönten Interactive Design Agentur CRASH!MEDIA. Craig arbeitet seit 1995 im Online-Geschäft und ist seit Gründung der Flash®-Gemeinde einer ihrer Schlüsselfiguren. Als Ausbilder, Kurator, Sprecher und Autor im Bereich der neuen Medien-Technologien hielt Craig bisher 20 internationale Vorträge zu Flash, ist Autor von und Beitragender zu sieben Büchern über Flash und betreute mehr als ein Dutzend Neue-Medien-Events, bei denen die besten Flash- und Interaktiv-Entwickler der Welt vorgestellt wurden. Seine Flash-Arbeit bei CRASH! wurde mehr als ein dutzend Mal ausgezeichnet und es wurde sowohl in der Presse als auch im Fernsehen darüber berichtet. Craig's interaktive Audio-Arbeit entwickelte sich zu der mehrfach ausgezeichneten Online-Musikanwendung Looplabs, die von Kunden wie Coca-Cola, Miller, Bacardi, Calvin Klein, Toyota, Sony und anderen verwendet wurde.

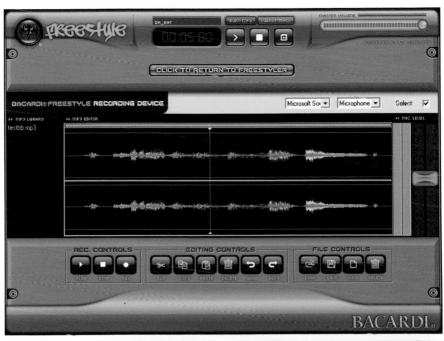

Interview:
Ed Motta

1) What's your view of the link between the Internet and music? Exploring new music, access to the widest variety possible of information sources, buying music, scores, etc.

I like to explain that the first time I accessed the Internet I cried since I knew I was experiencing what was undoubtedly the most important phenomenon of my generation. Ever since I was a child, I've been a "freaky information addict", I used to buy Japanese music catalogues, for example, even though I couldn't understand them, just to keep up with the new launches and keep in touch with the Japanese atmosphere. With the Internet, I now frenetically seek out thousands of artists from around the world. Denmark, Poland, Russia, Japan. The culture gap has been narrowed and that has changed my life.

2) As an artist, how do you use the Internet?

More specifically on my music. I spend the whole day on the Internet, tracking what's going on with my music, from New Zealand to Chile. I don't avoid the negative comments and of course that's not always so pleasant... Most of the time, however, the balance is positive. Better!

3) How do you relate to your fans over the Internet?

Although I can only answer a few e-mails, I read absolutely everything that's sent to my website. This contact improves the quality of the discussion and helps to downplay the myth of the untouchable artist. That's clear in my case, anyway, I don't think I'm so "special" as not to read the e-mails that people send to me. It's the least I can do, isn't it?

4) How do you think the Internet will change the music business?

I hope the change will be a democratic and artistically free change. If the record companies really do digitise all their material, it will be a great cultural advance.

5) What are the benefits of your website for you?

I disseminate my art, and the art of comic illustrator Edna Lopes – a fantastic artist, who is creator and designer of the site – all around the planet. That's truly fascinating.

6) What is your contribution to the site and how does it work?

I write a blog on rare discs, where visitors can hear the music in real time. And I'm continually working with Edna to keep the site updated.

7) What are the site's outstanding features (in other words, features that mustn't be lost)?

I don't really want to say it, but I think every page has its own surprise.

8) Do you listen to music live from the Internet? What equipment do you use?

When drinking my wines... I don't listen to my vinyl anymore, I've scratched a few of them. So I use iTunes, an optimum tool. From time to time, I go into shuffle mode, it's the best radio station in the world, the programmer has got incredible taste (laughs).

9) The music is still essentially the same. But how has the arrival of the digital age changed things for musicians?

Digital recordings have a timbre which I don't like, but the strong points compensate for this apparent technical weakness. Now, I use the computer to record and mix my discs; it is our reality, although I'm not a defender of the aesthetics of digital sound, even though I have 4 60 GB ipods.

Ed Motta is a Brazilian musician and composer, who navigates many styles of music and is well known for intellectual challenge. He lives in Rio de Janeiro and is a frequent visitor to the US, other areas of South America, Japan and Europe. <www.edmotta.com>

L'entretien :
Ed Motta

1) Le lien entre Internet et la musique, qu'est-ce que c'est pour vous ? Explorer de nouvelles formes de musiques, accéder à la plus large variété possible de sources d'information, acheter de la musique, des partitions, etc.

J'aime bien raconter que, la première fois que j'ai surfé sur Internet, j'étais très ému à l'idée d'expérimenter le plus important phénomène de ma génération. J'ai toujours été un "accroc de l'information", depuis l'enfance. Il m'arrivait souvent, par exemple, d'acheter des catalogues de musique japonaise dont je ne comprenais pas un traître mot, juste pour être courant des nouveaux lancements et rester en contact avec l'atmosphère japonaise. Avec Internet, maintenant, je cherche frénétiquement des milliers d'artistes dans le monde entier. Danemark, Pologne, Russie, Japon. Le fossé culturel s'est comblé et ça a changé ma vie.

2) En tant qu'artiste, utilisez-vous Internet ?

Oui, plus particulièrement pour ma propre musique. Je passe la journée sur Internet, à fureter de ci de là pour savoir ce qui se dit de ma musique, de la Nouvelle Zélande au Chili. Je n'évite pas les critiques et, bien entendu, ce n'est pas toujours très agréable... Mais l'un dans l'autre, le bilan est positif. Tant mieux !

3) Comment gardez-vous le contact avec vos fans sur Internet ?

Bien que je ne puisse répondre qu'à quelques courriels, je lis absolument tout ce qui arrive sur mon site. Ce contact améliore la qualité de la discussion et contribue à détruire le mythe de l'artiste intouchable. Pour moi c'est clair en tout cas, je ne me prends pas pour quelqu'un de si "spécial" que ça me dispenserait de lire les courriels que les gens m'envoient. C'est bien le moins que je puisse faire, non ?

4) En quoi Internet va-t-il changer l'industrie de la musique à votre avis ?

J'espère que le changement sera démocratique et libre, artistiquement parlant. Si les compagnies de disques numérisent vraiment tout le matériel, nous aurons fait un immense progrès culturel.

5) Quels sont les avantagesque vous rapporte votre site Web ?

Je diffuse mon art, et celui de l'illustratrice de BD Edna Lopes – une remarquable artiste, qui a conçu et dessiné le site– dans toute la planète. C'est vraiment extraordinaire.

6) En quoi contribuez-vous à ce site, et

comment fonctionne-t-il ?

J'écris un blog sur des disques rares que les visiteurs peuvent écouter en temps réel. Et je n'arrête pas de l'actualiser, en collaboration avec Edna.

7) Quelles sont les fonctions les plus remarquables du site (autrement, ce qu'il ne faut surtout pas rater)?

Je préfère ne pas le dire, mais je pense que chaque page réserve sa propre surprise.

8) Écoutez-vous de la musique live sur Internet ? Quel équipement utilisez-vous?

En buvant mes vins ... Je n'écoute plus mes vinyles, j'en ai rayé quelques-uns. Alors j'utilise iTunes, on ne fait pas mieux comme outil. De temps en temps, je vais sur shuffle mode, la meilleure station de radio du monde... le programmeur a un goût incroyable (rires).

9) La musique est en gros la même, mais peut-on dire que l'avénement de l'âge numérique a changé des choses pour les musiciens ?

Les enregistrements numériques ont une sonorité que je n'aime pas, mais il y a aussi des points forts qui compensent cette apparente faiblesse technique. Actuellement, j'utilise

l'ordinateur pour composer et mixer mes disques ; telle est notre réalité, bien que je ne sois pas favorable aux esthétiques de son numérique, et même si je possède 4 i-pods 60 GB.

Ed Motta, musicien et compositeur brésilien réputé pour son engagement intellectuel, navigue d'un style à l'autre. Il vit à Riu de Janeiro et fréquente régulièrement les USA, d'autres zones d'Amérique du Sud, le Japon et l'Europe. <www.edmotta.com>

Das Interview:
Ed Motta

1) Was denken Sie über die Verbindung von Internet und Musik? Die Möglichkeit der Erforschung neuer Musikrichtungen, Zugang zu einer großen Auswahl an Informationsquellen, Kaufen von Musik, Filmmusik etc.

Als ich zum ersten Mal Zugang zum Internet hatte, brach ich in Tränen aus. Ich wusste, dass ich gerade das zweifellos wichtigste Phänomen meiner Generation erlebte. Seit meiner Kindheit war ich ein "Informationssüchtiger". Obwohl ich sie nicht verstand, kaufte ich zum Beispiel regelmäßig japanische Musikkataloge, um mich einfach nur über die Neuveröffentlichungen auf dem Laufenden zu halten und mit der japanischen Atmosphäre in Verbindung zu bleiben. Über das Internet konnte ich nun frenetisch tausende von Künstlern überall auf der Welt ausfindig machen. Dänemark, Polen, Russland, Japan. Die Kluft zwischen den Kulturen hatte sich verringert und das hat mein Leben verändert.

2) Wie benutzen Sie das Internet als Künstler?

Besonders für meine eigene Musik. Ich verbringe den ganzen Tag im Internet und verfolge, was mit meiner Musik geschieht, von Neuseeland bis Chile. Ich vermeide dabei auch die negativen Kommentare nicht und das ist natürlich nicht immer so angenehm.....Meistens

ist die Bilanz aber positiv. Zum Glück!

3) Wie können Sie über das Internet Beziehungen zu Ihren Fans pflegen?

Obwohl ich nur ein paar e-mails beantworten kann, lese ich absolut alles, was zu meiner Website gesendet wird. Diese Kontakte verbessern die Auseinandersetzung mit meiner Musik und entkräften den Mythos des unnahbaren Künstlers. So ist es zumindest bei mir der Fall. Ich denke nicht, dass ich zu "besonders" bin, um die e-mails meiner Fans zu lesen. Das ist das Geringste, das ich tun kann, nicht wahr?

4) Wie wird das Internet Ihrer Meinung nach das Musikgeschäft verändern?

Ich hoffe, dass die Veränderung eine demokratische und künstlerisch freie Veränderung sein wird. Wenn die Plattenfirmen wirklich ihr gesamtes Material digitalisieren, wird das einen großen kulturellen Fortschritt bedeuten.

5) Welche Vorteile bietet Ihnen Ihre Website?

Ich kann über meine Website weltweit meine Kunst verbreiten sowie die Kunst der Comiczeichnerin Edna Lopes – eine phantastische Künstlerin und außerdem Schöpferin und Designerin meiner Website. Das ist wirklich

faszinierend.

6) Wie tragen Sie zu Ihrer Website bei und wie funktioniert sie?

Ich schreibe ein Blog auf seltene Disks, über das meine Besucher die Musik in Echtzeit hören können. Und ich arbeite ständig mit Edna zusammen, um die Website aktualisiert zu halten.

7) Welches sind die besonderen Merkmale der Website (mit anderen Worten, welche Merkmale sollten nicht verloren gehen)?

Ich möchte es eigentlich gar nicht sagen, doch ich denke, dass jede Seite etwas besonderes bietet.

8) Hören Sie Livemusik über das Internet? Welche Ausstattung verwenden Sie dazu?

Wenn ich meinen Wein trinke.... Ich höre meine Platten nicht mehr an, ich habe leider ein paar von ihnen zerkratzt. Daher benutze ich iTunes, ein optimales Tool. Von Zeit zu Zeit gehe ich in "Shuffle Mode", das ist der beste Radiosender der Welt. Der Programmgeber hat einen unglaublichen Geschmack (lacht).

9) Musik ist im Wesentlichen gleich geblieben. Doch welche Änderungen bringt der

Beginn des digitalen Zeitalters für die Musiker? Digitale Aufnahmen haben ein Timbre, das ich nicht mag. Doch die Vorteile kompensieren diese scheinbar technische Schwäche. Ich verwende den Computer, um meine Disks aufzunehmen und abzumischen; dies gehört zu unserer Realitätit, obwohl ich kein Fan der Ästhetik von digitalem Sound bin. Auch wenn ich vier 60 GB iPods besitze.

Ed Motta ist ein brasilianischer Musiker und Komponist, der sich mit vielen Musikstilen beschäftigt und für seine interlektuellen Herausforderungen bekannt ist. Er lebt in Rio de Janeiro und besucht regelmäßig die USA, andere südamerikanische Länder, Japan und Europa.

ABSOLUT KRAVITZ

SWEDEN

www.absolutkravitz.com

2006

Highlights

This fresh track was also remixed by ten of the world's leading producers like Little Louie Vega and Luny Tunes. Download the songs and videos for free. /// Ce morceau, d'une grande fraîcheur, est également remixé par les dix plus grands producteurs au monde, notamment Little Louie Vega et Luny Tunes. Téléchargez les chansons et les vidéos gratuitement. /// Diesen frischen Titel gibt es auch als Remix von zehn der weltführenden Produzenten, unter anderem Little Louie Vega und Luny Tunes. Der Download der Songs und Videos ist kostenlos.

Info

DESIGN AND PROGRAMMING: North Kingdom <www.northkingdom.com>. /// **TOOLS:** Macromedia Flash, Adobe Photoshop, 3D Studio Max, Adobe After Effects. /// **CONTENTS:** music, videos, interviews, wallpapers, podcast, vodcast. /// **DOWNLOAD:** music, videos, interviews, wallpapers, podcast, vodcast. /// **AWARDS:** FWA (Site of the Day). /// **COST:** 2000 hours.

ANNIE LENNOX

Highlights

She's literally the centre of her site. Exactly the way it should be. And she is the happy owner of a flash94 content management system to keep her story updated. /// Le centre du site c'est elle, littéralement. Et c'est exactement comme ça que ça doit être. D'autant qu'étant l'heureuse propriétaire d'un système de gestion de contenus flash94, elle peut actualiser son historique. /// Sie ist buchstäblich das Zentrum ihrer Site, und genau so sollte es sein. Und sie ist glückliche Besitzerin eines Flash94 Inhalt-Managementsystems, das für ständige Updates sorgt.

Info

DESIGN AND PROGRAMMING: group94 <www.group94.com>. /// TOOLS: Macromedia Freehand, Adobe Photoshop, Macromedia Flash. /// CONTENTS: news blog, photos, video-clips, music, biography, forum. /// COST: 5 weeks.

ALICIA KEYS

USA
2005

www.aliciakeys.com

Highlights

Alicia Keys is able to upload photos taken with her fan base using our custom designed CMS and can also upload her personal writings to the website while on tour. /// En utilisant notre CSM personnalisé, Alicia Keys peut aussi bien télécharger vers le site des photos prises avec son fan-club qu'y accrocher dans son journal les réflexions qu'elle rédige en cours de tournée. /// Alicia Keys verwendet unser anwendungsspezifisches CMS und kann dadurch Fotos von sich mit ihren Fans hochladen sowie ihre persönlichen Beiträge auf der Website, wenn sie auf Tour ist.

Info

DESIGN: Bukwild <www.bukwild.com>. /// PROGRAMMING: Jeff Toll and Robert Reinhard <www.bukwild.com>. /// TOOLS: CMS, Javascript, XML, Oracle, PHP, Adobe Photoshop, Macromedia Flash, Adobe Illustrator. /// CONTENTS: news, tours, photos, fan photos, journal, downloads, audio, events, links, buy, media, community, bio, shows, appearances, books, movies, music, organizations. /// DOWNLOAD: Mp3 player, wallpapers, screensavers, ecard. /// AWARDS: e-creative.net. /// COST: 100 hours.

ALL OF THE ABOVE

www.all-of-the-above.com

Highlights

These guys play Creative Covers, this is a "LIVE" band, therefore the whole website uses extensive live icons such as flightcases, stage lights and P.A. sound systems. /// Ils jouent Creative Covers, c'est un groupe "LIVE", d'où l'utilisation, dans tout le site, d'images de malles de voyage, de lumières de scène et de sons PA. /// Diese Jungs spielen Creative Covers. Es handelt sich um eine "LIVE"-Band, daher verwendet die gesamte Website umfangreiche Live-Symbole wie zum Beispiel Flightcases, Bühnenlichter und Lautsprecher.

Info

DESIGN: Hypnotized Design <www.hypnotized.org>. /// PROGRAMMING: Hypno Seven <www.hypno7.com>. /// TOOLS: Adobe Photoshop, Macromedia Flash. /// CONTENTS: photos, animations, sound effects. /// DOWNLOAD: hi-res photos, Mp3, wallpapers. /// AWARDS: NewWebPick, Ades Award, Plastic Pilot, Yellow Pimiento, Pixelmakers, Strangefruits, and more. /// COST: 40-50 hours.

Highlights

In accordance with Arturo Fuentes' composing method (fragmentation, density, formant) countless squared fragments appear from the distance and populate a multi-dimensional soundspace. /// En concordance avec la méthode de composition d'Arturo Fuentes (fragmentation, densité, micro activité), venus du fond de l'écran, d'innombrables fragments quadrangulaires se matérialisent et viennent peupler un espace sonore multidimensionnel. /// In Übereinstimmung mit Arturo Fuentes' Methode des Komponierens (Fragmentierung, Dichte, Formant) erscheinen von weitem zahllose quadratische Fragmente und bestücken eine multidimensionale Klangwelt.

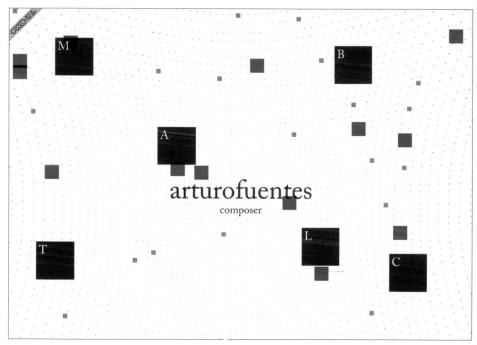

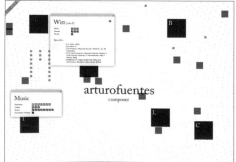
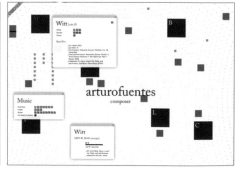

Info

DESIGN: Transporter Concept.Print.Web. <www.transporter.at>. /// PROGRAMMING: Rainer Fabrizi (Transporter). /// TOOLS: Macromedia Flash, Macromedia Dreamweaver, Adobe Photoshop, Macromedia Freehand, Soundedit, iTunes, PHP, mySQL, cargo*CMS, Javascript, Transmit. /// CONTENTS: fragments in soundspace, texts, photos, music scores, sound samples, video-clips. /// DOWNLOAD: biography, texts, photos, information/scores/sound samples/videos of each music piece. /// AWARDS: FWA (Site of the Day), Nominated for Tirolissimo (Tyrolean advertising award). /// COST: 225 hours.

ATLANTIC RECORDS

UK
2004

www.atlanticrecords.co.uk

Highlights

It allows users to access latest releases, news and back catalogue material of Atlantic's artists, as well as hosting a streaming radio station of their hits. /// Ses utilisateurs peuvent accéder aux nouveautés des stars d'Atlantic, à des infos, aux produits de 'back catalogue', ainsi qu'à une station de radio en streaming diffusant leurs tubes. /// Sie ermöglicht den Benutzern, auf die neusten Veröffentlichungen der Atlantic-Künstler zuzugreifen sowie auf ältere Werke und bietet einen Internet-Radiosender mit ihren Hits.

Info

DESIGN: Prezence UK <www.prezence.co.uk>. /// TOOLS: CMS, php, Adobe Photoshop, Macromedia Flash, Macromedia Dreamweaver. /// CONTENTS: full catalogue with artist pages, full discography, mobile content, jukebox, buy album/tracks online. /// COST: 160 hours

ATLANTIC STREET

UK
2005

www.atlanticstreet.co.uk

Highlights Users can buy tracks, get news and information on their favourites, sign up for the label's newsletter and participate in the forums. /// Les visiteurs peuvent acheter des morceaux, lire des nouvelles et des infos sur leurs artistes favoris, s'abonner à la newsletter du label et participer aux forums. /// Benutzer können Musiktitel kaufen, Nachrichten und Informationen über ihre Lieblingskünstler abrufen, den Newsletter abbonieren und sich in die Foren einloggen.

Info DESIGN: Prezence UK <www.prezence.co.uk>. /// TOOLS: CMS, php, Adobe Photoshop, Macromedia Flash, Macromedia Dreamweaver. /// CONTENTS: full catalogue with artist pages, full discography, mobile content, jukebox, buy album/tracks online. /// COST: 100 hours.

DECIBEL OUTDOOR
www.b2s.nl/decibel

Highlights

The site engages you in a full blown experience of the outdoor area where the festival will take place. You are virtually taken from one area to the next in a non-linear fashion. /// Ce Web vous invite à parcourir dans ses moindres détails le site où doit avoir lieu le festival. Vous êtes virtuellement conduit d'un endroit à l'autre, sans solution de continuité. /// Die Website bietet dem Benutzer das volle Erlebnis der Festival-Location. Man wird virtuell auf nichtlineare Art und Weise von einem Ort zum anderen befördert.

Info

DESIGN AND PROGRAMMING: thePharmacy <www.thepharmacy-media.com>. /// TOOLS: 3D Studio Max, Adobe Photoshop, Adobe Illustrator, PHP, MySQL, Macromedia Flash. /// CONTENTS: 3D animated navigation, video, audio clips, audio player, voice overs. /// DOWNLOAD: 2 radio commercials, 1 TV commercial. /// COST: 120 hours.

Highlights

AgencyNet created a fourth generation web site with associated applications that feature 4 genres of music, a robust sample bank, an entirely new 8-channel online mixer application and over 400 custom music loops. /// AgencyNet a créé un Web de la quatrième génération, avec une application associée qui comprend 4 genres de musique, une banque de samplers bien remplie, une application de mixage on-line 8 pistes entièrement nouvelle et plus de 400 boucles musicales personnalisées. /// AgencyNet schaffte eine Website der vierten Generation und verknüpfte sie mit Anwendungen, die vier Genre der Musik anbieten sowie gute Samples, eine 8-Kanal Online-Mixer Anwendung und über 400 Musikwiederholungen.

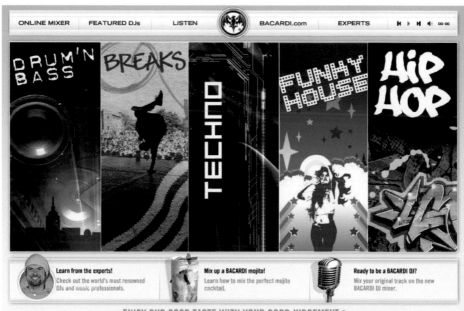

Info

DESIGN AND PROGRAMMING: AgencyNet <www.agencynet.com>. /// TOOLS: XML, CMS, SQL, .NET, Adobe Photoshop, Macromedia Flash.

BACARDI FREESTYLE

www.bacardilive.com/freestyle

Highlights

This site allowed for the first-ever online MC battle. Users could create custom audio tracks as backing and then lay down their raps/vocals on top with a microphone and ultimately submit them online. /// Ce site a accueilli la première MC battle on-line. Ses utilisateurs pouvaient créer leurs propres backing tracks audio et, avec un micro, rapper ou mettre des voix en surimpression, puis présenter le tout on-line. /// Diese Website ermöglichte zum allerersten Mal einen online MC Wettkampf. Benutzer konnten anwendungsspezifische Audiotitel kreieren, mit einem Mikrophon ihre Raps/Stimmen darüber legen und online zum Besten geben.

Info

DESIGN AND PROGRAMMING: CRASH!MEDIA <www.crashmedia.com>. /// TOOLS: Macromedia Flash, Adobe Photoshop. /// CONTENTS: sound loops and samples. /// DOWNLOAD: save recordings to MP3. /// AWARDS: FITC (Best Audio). /// COST: 400 hours.

BECK

www.beck.com

2005

UK

Highlights

Taking its origin from the 19th century Viennese Theatre, we developed a virtual mechanical version of it, using our own photography of sculptures made up of tapes and CD cases. /// À partir de l'idée d'un théâtre viennois du XIXème siècle, nous en avons mis au point une version virtuelle mécanique, en utilisant nos propres photos de sculptures fabriquées avec des boîtiers de cassettes et de CD. /// Der Ursprung stammt aus dem Wiener Theater des 19. Jahrhunderts. Wir entwickelten davon eine virtuelle mechanische Version und verwendeten dabei unsere eigenen Fotos von Skulpturen, die aus Tonbändern und CD-Hüllen gefertigt sind.

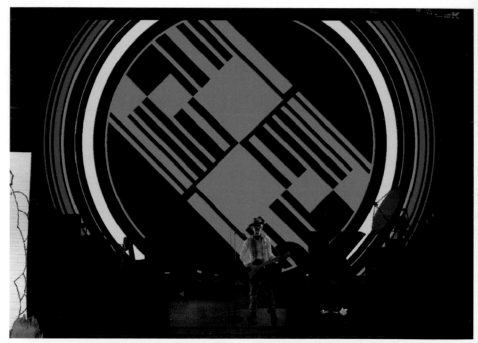

Info

DESIGN: Hi-ReS! <www.hi-res.net>. /// PRODUCER: Nicky Cameron. /// ART DIRECTOR: Florian Schmitt. /// DESIGNER: Tommi Eberwein, Carl Burgess. /// INTERACTIVE DESIGNER: Tommi Eberwein, Carl Burgess. /// RICH MEDIA DEVELOPER: Dan Wright. /// TOOLS: Adobe Photoshop, Adobe Illustrator, Macromedia Flash. /// CONTENTS: photo, video-clips, tour, animation. /// DOWNLOAD: samples, tracks, Mp3, wallpaper. /// AWARDS: D&AD Award.

BENZ & MD
www.benzandmd.com

CANADA
2003

Highlights

The site features custom action-scripting, photography and a selection of audio tracks from Benz&MD for users to preview. /// De l'action-scripting personnalisée, des photos et des sélections audio de Benz&MD en avant-première pour les utilisateurs, voici ce que propose ce site. /// Die Website bietet ihren Besuchern eine Vorschau an Aktionsdrehs, Fotos und Audio-Auswahlen von Benz&MD.

Info

DESIGN: Velocity Studio & Associates <www.velocitystudio.com>. /// **PROGRAMMING:** Eric Vardon & Jonathan Coe (Velocity Studio & Associates). /// **TOOLS:** CMS, php, Adobe Photoshop, Macromedia Flash. /// **CONTENTS:** photo, audio-clips, animation. /// **DOWNLOAD:** tracks Real Player, Mp3. /// **COST:** 2 months.

BERNARD GAVILAN

www.bernardgavilan.com

Highlights

Bernard Gavilan. Bitch. Sinner. Style icon and Fashion Freak. Turning up the volume. Polyester beats. /// Bernard Gavilan. Look bitch. 'Sinner'. Style icône et Fashion Freak. Monter le son. Pulsations polyester. /// Bernard Gavilan. Bitch. Sinner. Stilikone und Modefreak. Laut. Polyester Beats.

Info

DESIGN AND PROGRAMMING: Milk and Cookies <www.milkandcookies.be>. /// **TOOLS:** Adobe Photoshop, Adobe Illustrator, Adobe After Effects, Macromedia Flash, Final Cut Pro. /// **CONTENTS:** photos, music, video, bio, etc. /// **DOWNLOAD:** Mp3, videos. /// **COST:** 1 month.

BILLY HARVEY MUSIC

www.billyharveymusic.com

2004

Highlights Finishing it alive and getting to build something real. /// Comment donner de la vivacité aux finitions, et construire quelque chose de vrai. /// Geschafft, und nun wird etwas reales gebaut.

Info **DESIGN:** sofake <www.sofake.com>. /// **TOOLS:** ink-jet printer, cardstock, scissors, tape, digital camera, Macromedia Flash, Adobe Photoshop. /// **CONTENTS:** multimedia. /// **DOWNLOAD:** Billy Harvey source. /// **AWARDS:** Best Music Site SXSW Interactive 2005, FWA, Bombshock. /// **COST:** 3 months.

BLEEP

Highlights

A big technical achievement. /// Une énorme réussite technique. /// Eine großartige technische Leistung.

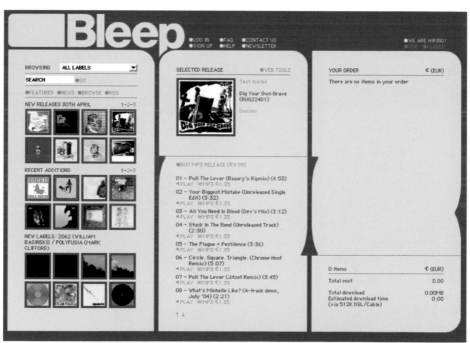

Info

DESIGN: The Designers Republic <www.thedesignersrepublic.com>. /// PROGRAMMING: Kleber Design Ltd. <www.kleber.net>. /// TOOLS: Adobe Photoshop, Macromedia Flash, php, HTML, CMS. /// CONTENTS: digital downloads shop. /// DOWNLOAD: Mp3. /// AWARDS: (Shortlisted) Best Digital Music Store, Music Week Awards 2006 / Best Music Website, Webby Awards 2004. /// COST: 6 months.

BLINK 182
www.blink182.com

Highlights

To make the Blink site sticky for its youthful audience, Domani produced a secure "interactive jukebox", an online audio player that played upcoming tracks while preventing downloads. /// Pour que Blink colle à son audience jeune, Domani a mis au point un "jukebox interactif" sécurisé, un lecteur audio on-line qui reproduit les nouveautés tout en prévenant les téléchargements. /// Um die Blink-Website für ihr junges Publikum attraktiv zu machen, produzierte Domani eine sichere "interaktive Jukebox", ein Online-Audioplayer, der neue Musiktitel spielte, ohne Downloads zuzulassen.

Info

DESIGN AND PROGRAMMING: Domani Studios <www.domanistudios.com>. /// TOOLS: Macromedia Flash, Proprietary CMS, streaming audio. /// CONTENTS: streaming music; news and events; community area; alien shooting game. /// DOWNLOAD: artist's songs and special tracks; wallpapers; application themes and skins; video interviews and concert footage.

BLUEPRINT STUDIOS

UK

www.blueprint-studios.com

2005

Highlights Built with love and lots of analogue meets digital trickery, sound and image fuse together to make a unique site for a recording studio. /// Construit avec amour et tout autant d'ingéniosité numérique du meilleur aloi ; sons et images fusionnent et produisent ainsi un site unique pour un studio d'enregistrement. /// **Eine mit viel Liebe gebaute Website, bei der Analogtechnik auf digitale Tricks trifft. Klänge und Bilder verschmelzen und schaffen eine einzigartige Seite für ein Aufnahmestudio.**

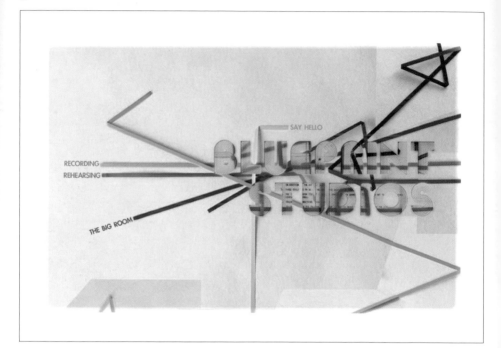

Info DESIGN: magneticNorth <www.magneticN.co.uk>. /// TOOLS: Macromedia Flash, paper ribbons, digital Camera, Adobe Photoshop, XML, ASP, mini moog, flute, harmonica, bassoon, accordian, piano, Pro-Tools, pencils, paper. /// CONTENTS: words and pictures. /// AWARDS: Design Week Awards 2006.

BOB SCHNEIDER MUSIC

USA/UK
2003

www.bobschneidermusic.com

This was the first wefail site for an actual client (ever) with Bob having us come on stage at a show and letting us throw down a wefail freestyle rap jam in front of a sold out Bob Schneider crowd of nearly 12,000 people /// C'est aussi le (tout) premier réalisé en wefail pour un client actuel. Bob nous a fait venir sur scène lors d'un de ses concerts à guichets fermés, et il nous a laissé mettre en boîte un rap freestyle wefail devant une foule de 12000 personnes. /// Und sie war auch die allererste Wefail-Site für einen wirklichen Kunden. Bob ließ uns während einer Show auf die Bühne kommen und ließ uns ein Wefail Freestyle Rap Jam vor einem ausverkauften Bob Schneider-Konzert von nahezu 12.000 Personen zeigen.

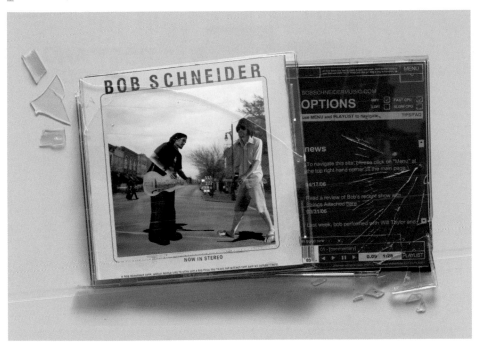

DESIGN: wefail <www.wefail.com>. /// TOOLS: Macromedia Flash, Adobe Photoshop. /// CONTENTS: multimedia. /// AWARDS: Best Music Site SXSW Interactive 2004, FWA. /// COST: 3 months.

MUSIC SITES · 79

BOST & BIM

www.bostandbim.com

Highlights

This is a reggae website. It's made to make you discover the universe of Bost&Bim listening to there music and exploring there place of work: the studio! enjoy! /// Il s'agit d'un site de reggae, conçu de manière à vous faire découvrir l'univers de Bost&Bim en écoutant leur musique et en explorant l'endroit où travaille le groupe : le studio! Amusez-vous bien ! /// Dies ist eine Reggae-Website. Sie wurde gemacht, damit du das Universum von Bost&Bim erforschen, ihre Musik hören und ihren Arbeitsplatz entdecken kannst: das Studio! Viel Spaß dabei!

Info

DESIGN AND PROGRAMMING: Zenkilla. /// TOOLS: Adobe Photoshop, Adobe Illustrator, Macromedia Flash, Macromedia Dreamweaver. /// CONTENTS: Music, discographie, biography and goodies. /// DOWNLOAD: Patchlist. /// COST: 90 hours.

CARMEN AND CAMILLE

www.carmenandcamille.com

Highlights

We filmed the characters the converted them into flash giving real movement and life-like appearance to the audience. There are 8-9 layers of different animated times in the intro yet it is only 2.8 MB. /// Nous avons filmé les personnages, puis les avons convertis en Flash en leur donnant le mouvement et l'apparence d'une audience vivante. L'intro comporte 8 à 9 calques de différents temps animés, et ne pèse que 2.8 MB. /// Wir filmten die Leute, wandelten dies in Flash um und fügten die echten Bewegungen und das naturgetreue Aussehen des Publikums hinzu. Trotz 8-9 Schichten mit verschieden animierten Zeiten im Intro hat es nur 2.8 MB.

■ FULL SCREEN
■ NORMAL WINDOW

TWIN SPIN music

Carmen and Camille © 2006

Info

DESIGN AND PROGRAMMING: GreatExposures <www.greatexposures.com>. /// TOOLS: Macromedia Flash, Adobe Photoshop, Adobe Premiere, Adobe Audition, PHP, XHTML, Actionscript, XML. /// CONTENTS: intro animation, virtual stage. /// COST: $15,000.

CESS MUSIC

Highlights

Minimal design crosses minimal techno. Smooth animations emphasize the music. Worldmap. /// Rencontre entre un design minimaliste et de la techno minimaliste. Une animation délicate met en valeur la musique. Carte du monde. /// Minimales Design kreuzt minimale Technologie. Weiche Animationen betonen die Musik. Weltkarte.

Info

DESIGN AND PROGRAMMING: Huy Dieu (GOOQ) <www.gooq.de>. /// TOOLS: CMS, php, Adobe Photoshop, Macromedia Freehand, Macromedia Flash. /// CONTENTS: photo, playlist, animation, streaming mp3, gallery, news, about, dates, diary, links, press downloads. /// DOWNLOAD: press images, press text files. /// COST: 14 days.

CHRISTOPHER LAWRENCE

www.christopherlawrence.com

Highlights

Watch video clips from Christopher Lawrence's worldwide live shows. Check out video and audio clips of Christopher Lawrence's hottest tracks. 3D graphics and sequences were created by 2Advanced Studios. /// Regardez les vidéoclips des performances en direct de Christopher Lawrence dans le monde entier. Consultez ses clips vidéo et audio de ses morceaux les plus chauds. Graphiques et séquences 3D créés par 2Advanced Studios. /// Videoclips von Christopher Lawrence's weltweiten Live-Shows. Video- und Audio-Clips von Christopher Lawrence's heißesten Titeln. 3D-Graphiken und Sequenzen von 2Advanced Studios.

Info

DESIGN: Eric Jordan (2Advanced Studios) <www.2advanced.com>. /// TOOLS: Macromedia Flash, HTML, PHP, Cinema 4D. /// CONTENTS: video, photo, audio. /// DOWNLOAD: video, photo, audio. /// AWARDS: Outstanding Website Award 2004 WMA Webaward Competition, 2005 Webby Awards (Music Category), 2005 SXSW Web Awards (Music Category). /// COST: 80 hours.

COLUMBIA RECORDS

www.columbia.co.uk

Highlights

Big site, very short turnaround. /// Grand site, se renouvelle sans cesse. /// Große Website, sehr schnelle Updates.

Info

DESIGN AND PROGRAMMING: Kleber Design Ltd. <www.kleber.net>. /// TOOLS: Adobe Photoshop, Macromedia Flash, php, HTML, CMS. /// CONTENTS: label news, artist biographies, releases, audio and video previews. /// COST: 2 weeks.

CULTURE CLUB

www.cultureclub.be

Highlights

"The hippest club in the world" - The Times. /// "Le club le plus 'hip' du monde" - The Times. /// "Der hippeste Club der Welt" (The Times).

Info

DESIGN AND PROGRAMMING: Milk and Cookies <www.milkandcookies.be>. /// **TOOLS:** Adobe Photoshop, Adobe Illustrator, Macromedia Flash. /// **CONTENTS:** all info you need. /// **COST:** 3 weeks.

DANIEL BEDINGFIELD

www.danielbedingfield.com

Highlights

Daniel Bedingfield's serene and uncomplicated pop sound was an inspiration for his official UK website. This easy-to-navigate site boasts stunning photography, as well as access to the latest news and tour info for the true fan. /// La pop sereine et sans complication de Daniel Bedingfield inspire son site officiel britannique. Ce site de navigation facile offre au véritable fan de stupéfiantes photos, ainsi qu'un accès aux dernières news et infos sur les tournées. /// Daniel Bedingfield's heiterer und unkomplizierter Pop-Sound inspiriert seine offizielle Website in der UK. Die einfach zu navigierende Seite bietet umwerfende Fotos sowie Zugang zu den neusten Nachrichten und Toureninfos für den wahren Fan.

DESIGN: Prezence UK <www.prezence.co.uk>. /// **TOOLS:** Php, Mysql, xHTML, CMS, CSS, Javascript, XML, CMS, Adobe Photoshop, Macromedia Flash, Macromedia Dreamweaver. /// **CONTENTS:** news, audio samples, photo galleries, video streams, forum, ringtones. /// **DOWNLOAD:** members only exclusive downloads. /// **COST:** 80 hours.

DB RECORDINGS
www.dbrecordings.com

Highlights

The highlight of the site is its slick interface design and dynamic mp3 and video player. /// Le trait marquant du site est un design brillant avec interface, mp3 dynamique et lecteur vidéo. /// Die Highlights dieser Website bestehen in einem geschickten Interface-Design sowie in einem dynamischen MP3- und Video-Player.

Info

DESIGN AND PROGRAMMING: Webshocker <www.webshocker.net>. /// TOOLS: Macromedia Flash, Adobe Photoshop, 3D Studio Max. /// CONTENTS: photo, video-clips, Mp3. /// DOWNLOAD: photo, video-clips, Mp3. /// AWARDS: TINY, King for a Week, Crossmind, Absolute Designer, etc. /// COST: 100 hours.

DIET STRYCHNINE RECORDS

www.dietstrychninerecords.com

Highlights

This hockney inspired design offers a fairly bare bones approach. The imagery is limited, the text is ASCII-based making the audio offerings on the site the focus. /// Ce design inspire par Hockney offre une assez bonne approche en barebone. L'imagerie est limitée, le texte est en ASCII, faisant de l'offre audio le centre du site. /// Dieses von Hockney inspirierte Design bietet eine ziemlich minimale Annäherung. Das Bildmaterial ist limitiert und der ASCII-basierte Text rückt die Audioelemente in das Zentrum der Website.

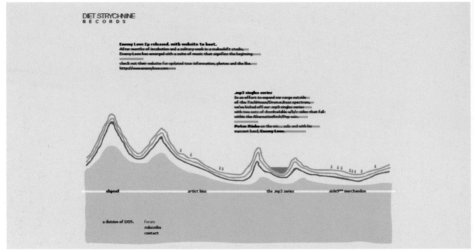

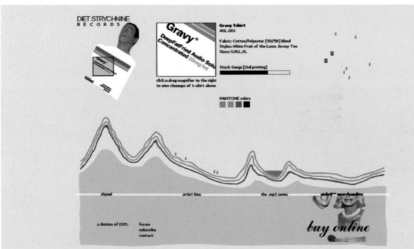

Info

DESIGN: Sacha Sedriks for DS9 Corp <www.dietstrychnine.com>. /// **PROGRAMMING:** Sacha Sedriks <www.artificialarea.com>. /// **TOOLS:** Macromedia Flash, Adobe Photoshop. /// **CONTENTS:** online store selling records, cds and merchandise. band photos, quicktime movie of performances, non-downloadable streaming audio. /// **DOWNLOAD:** MP3 EP downloads. /// **AWARDS:** 365: AIGA Year in Design 25. /// **COST:** 125 hours.

DIXIE CHICKS

www.dixiechicks.com

Interesting navigation concept, a very simplistic but overall atmospheric website. /// Concept de navigation intéressant, site Web très simple, mais atmosphère d'ensemble assez réussie. /// Interessantes Navigationskonzept, sehr simplistische aber schöne und atmosphärische Website.

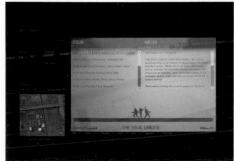

Info DESIGN: wefail <www.wefail.com>. /// TOOLS: Adobe Photoshop, Macromedia Flash. /// CONTENTS: multimedia.

DWELE

www.dwele.net

Highlights

We combined his portraits against a series of cityscapes, revealing them in translucent layers to achieve a mysterious feel. The result is an artful site that is inspired by his understated modern elegance. /// Nous avons associé des photos de lui et des séries de paysages urbains, en les révélant par couchage translucide afin de créer une impression de mystère. Le résultat est un site vraiment artistique, inspiré par l'élégance naturelle implicite de Dwele. /// Wir stellten sein Porträt in einer Serie von Stadtlandschaften dar und zeigten diese in transluzenten Schichten, um eine geheimnisvolle Atmosphäre zu schaffen. Das Ergebnis ist eine kunstvolle Site, die von Dwele's dezenten und modernen Eleganz inspiriert ist.

Info

DESIGN AND PROGRAMMING: Fahrenheit Studio <www.fahrenheit.com>. /// **TOOLS:** Macromedia Flash, Adobe Photoshop, Adobe Illustrator, CMS, HTML. /// **CONTENTS:** photos, audio/video, tour, bio, journal, animation, message board. /// **DOWNLOAD:** photos, wallpapers, buddy icons. /// **AWARDS:** Horizon Interactive Award. /// **COST:** 100 hours.

ED MOTTA

www.edmotta.com

Highlights

Multilingual website with personalized illustrations, videos, and top Brazilian music and Jazz to enjoy. /// Site en plusieurs langues avec des illustrations personnalisées, des vidéos, et ce qu'on fait de mieux en matière de musique brésilienne et de jazz. /// Multilinguale Website mit personalisierten Illustrationen, Videos, brasilianischer Topmusik und Jazz zum genießen.

Info

DESIGN: Edna Lopes <www.ednalopes.com>. /// PROGRAMMING: Bruno Novaes e Débora Nóbrega <www.contatodireto.com> /// TOOLS. html, Macromedia Flash. /// CONTENTS: illustrated discography, sound tracks, history, blog (audio), articles and interviews (from 1987 till today), lists of favourites, agenda, videos, radio with Ed Motta as a host and programmer, photos and articles writen by Ed Motta about wine & music for brazilian newspapers, memorabilia, rare photos and illustrations. /// DOWNLOAD: photos, video, Mp3. /// COST: 800 hours.

EFFET PLACEBO
www.effet-placebo.fr

Highlights Exclusive audio and video content. The contents of the website is fully manageable. The Webdesign has been taken from the artwork and enhanced to give the user the most immersive atmosphere. /// Contenu audio et vidéo exclusif. Tous les contenus y sont entièrement administrables. Le design, tiré de la maquette, a été agrandi pour donner au visiteur le sentiment de plonger dans une atmosphère à part. /// Exklusive Audio- und Video-Inhalte, die leicht zu handhaben sind. Das Webdesign lehnt sich an die künstlerische Darstellung an und wurde weiterentwickelt, um dem Besucher eine eindringliche Atmosphäre zu bieten.

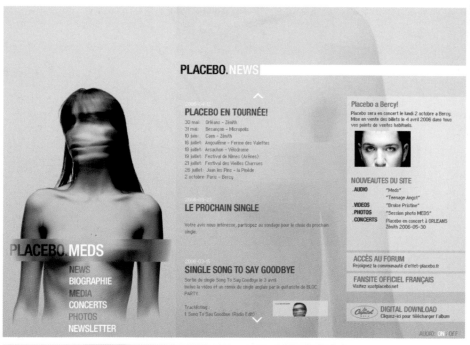

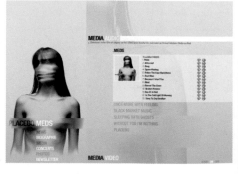

Info DESIGN: Etienne Desclides (Soleil Noir) <www.soleilnoir.net>. /// PROGRAMMING: Maxime Montegnies (Soleil Noir). /// PROJECT MANAGER: Olivier Marchand (Soleil Noir). /// TOOLS: Adobe Photoshop, Macromedia Flash, XML, Php. /// CONTENTS: news, photo, video-clips, tour, biography, forum. /// COST: 3 weeks.

EMI MUSIC FRANCE

www.emi.fr

Highlights

"Wide" style design. Original and ergonomic navigation. All content on this website is fully manageable using an advanced Content Management System based on RSS Technology. /// Design "Widestyle". Originale navigation ergonomique. Le contenu du site est entièrement administrable grâce à un CSM avancé utilisant la technologie RSS. /// "Wide"-Style Design. Ursprüngliche und ergonomische Navigation. Durch ein fortschrittliches Inhalt-Managementsystem, das auf RSS-Technologie basiert, sind alle Inhalte dieser Website gut überschaubar.

Info

DESIGN: Alexandre Tyack (Soleil Noir) <www.soleilnoir.net>. /// PROGRAMMING: Morgane Peinado, Maxime Montegnies (Soleil Noir). /// PROJECT MANAGER: Benjamin Laugel (Soleil Noir). /// TOOLS: Adobe Photoshop, Macromedia Flash, XML, Php. /// CONTENTS: artist, news, calendar, e-shop, photo, video-clips, web radio, tour, history. /// AWARDS: FWA, Macromedia (Featured Site), TINY (Site of the Week). /// COST: 4 weeks.

EMINEM

www.eminem.com

Meeting Eminem. Me and Martin having cameos in his video for "when I'm gone". /// Rencontre avec Eminem. Moi et Martin jouons un petit rôle dans son clip vidéo pour "When I'm gone". /// Hier trifft man Eminem. Martin und ich tauchen kurz in seinem Video für "When I'm gone" auf.

DESIGN: wefail <www.wefail.com>. /// TOOLS: Macromedia Flash, Adobe Photoshop. /// CONTENTS: multimedia. /// AWARDS: Best Music Site SXSW Interactive 2006, FWA. /// COST: 3-4 weeks.

ENEMY LOVE

www.enemylove.com

Highlights

The full bleed video loop backdrop is something we had never seen before. Ultra updatable by people (ELove members) that know next to nothing of web technologies. /// Quant au loop vidéo franc-bord qui y fait office de toile de fond, nous n'avions jamais rien vu de pareil. Ultra actualisable, y compris par quelqu'un (ELove members) qui ne saurait pratiquement rien des technologies du Web. /// Der phantastische Videohintergrund ist etwas, was wir noch nie zuvor gesehen hatten. Sehr leichte Updates für Leute (ELove-Clubmitglieder), die so gut wie nichts über Web-Technology wissen.

Info

DESIGN: Sacha Sedriks for Diet Strychnine Corp. <www.dietstrychnine.com>. /// PROGRAMMING: Sacha Sedriks <www.dietstrychninerecords.com>. /// TOOLS: Adobe Photoshop, Adobe Illustrator, Macromedia Flash, Quicktime Video. /// CONTENTS: photos, video-clips, audio, tour information, blog entry. /// DOWNLOAD: entire EP, press photos. /// COST: 80 hours, with constant additions.

ESOUNDS

www.esounds.co.za

Highlights

It allows users to access the latest news, releases, competitions and DVDs surrounding their favourite artists as well as supplying links to the artists' own sites. /// Il permet aux utilisateurs d'accéder aux dernières nouvelles, sorties, concours et DVD relatifs à leurs artistes favoris, et fournit des liens vers les sites personnels de ceux-ci. /// Sie ermöglicht den Besuchern Zugang zu den neusten Nachrichten, Veröffentlichungen, Wettbewerben und DVDs rund um ihre Lieblingskünstler und bietet Links zu den eigenen Websites der Künstler.

Info

DESIGN: Prezence SA <www.prezence.co.za>. /// TOOLS: Php, MySql, xHTML, CSS, Javascript, XML, CMS, Adobe Photoshop, Macromedia Flash, Macromedia Dreamweaver. /// CONTENTS: news, releases (DVDs and CDs), album information including tracklistings and links to buy online, tracksamplers on releases, site jukebox, competitions, artist biographies. /// DOWNLOAD: wallpapers, screensavers, interactive desktops. /// COST: 200 hours.

FACING NEW YORK
www.facingnewyork.com

USA
2003

Highlights

Looking at it years later and laughing and thinking it's a pretty dopey site /// Le voir au bout de tant d'années, on se prend à rire et à penser que c'est vraiment de la sacrée bonne came de site. /// Jahre später sieht man auf die Website, lacht und denkt, es ist eine ziemlich gute Website.

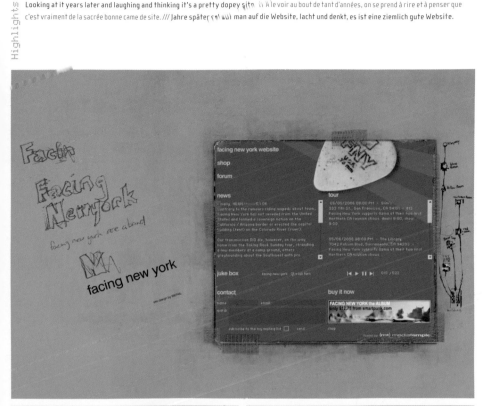

DESIGN: wefail <www.wefail.com>. /// TOOLS: Macromedia Flash, Adobe Photoshop. /// CONTENTS: multimedia. /// AWARDS: FWA. /// COST: 3 months.

FAITHLESS

www.faithless.co.uk

Highlights

Faithless are known for their opinionated lyrics so we made the lyrics a focal point for users syncing the audio with bold typography as part of the navigation and overall experience. /// Faithless est connu pour ses paroles engagées, c'est donc sur les textes que le site a été axé pour les utilisateurs, en synchronisant l'audio avec une typographie en gras, conçue comme une partie de la navigation et de l'expérience d'ensemble. /// Faithless ist bekannt für ihre eigenwilligen Texte. Daher setzten wir die Texte ins Zentrum der Site und synchronisierten die Audio-Elemente mit kühner Typographie als Teil der Navigation und des Gesamterlebnisses.

Info

DESIGN AND PROGRAMMING: de-construct <www.de-construct.com>. /// TOOLS: Adobe Photoshop, Macromedia Flash. /// CONTENTS: photos, video, editorial, mobile content. /// DOWNLOAD: video, wallpapers, Mp3. /// AWARDS: Best Dance Music Site, Dance Music Awards 2005. /// COST: 5 weeks.

Highlights

Play along to full length tracks from the 1980's with a set of interactive drums. Choose from 3 fresh kits to play with. Classic dog bark sample included. /// Un site qui tient en haleine avec des morceaux entiers, depuis les années 80, et un jeu de drums interactifs. Faites votre choix parmi 3 kits de jeu. Sampler d'aboiement de chien inclus : un classique. /// Ganzaufnahmen von Musiktiteln der 80er Jahre mit einer Reihe von interaktiven Drums. Der Besucher kann zwischen drei guten Ausstattungen wählen und damit spielen, einschließlich mit einem klassichen Hundegebell-Sample.

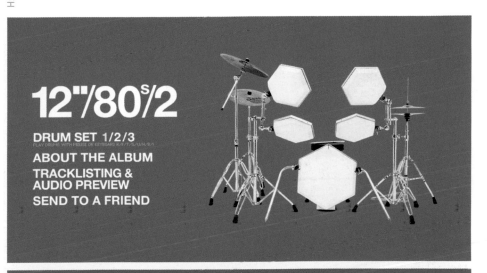

Info

DESIGN AND PROGRAMMING: Dom Murphy (TAK!) <www.taktak.net>. /// TOOLS: Adobe Photoshop, Macromedia Fireworks, Macromedia Flash. /// CONTENTS: audio. /// COST: 40 hours.

FILIGROOVES

www.filigrooves.com

Highlights Featuring the interface of a vintage reel-to-reel tape recorder, this web site builds a wonderfully nostalgic atmosphere around the presentation of some really funky buyout music. /// Comprenant l'interface d'un vieux magnétophone à bande, ce site instaure une merveilleuse atmosphère de nostalgie autour de la présentation d'un véritable funk buyout. /// Durch das Interface eines Vintage Reel-to-Reel Tonbandgerätes schafft diese Website eine wundervoll nostalgische Atmosphäre für die Präsentation einiger wirklich irren Musiktitel.

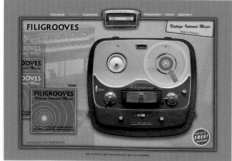 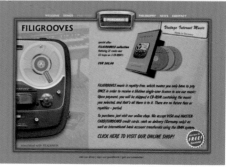

Info DESIGN AND PROGRAMMING: Filigrafix Media Design <www.filigrafix.de>. /// TOOLS: Macromedia Flash, Adobe Photoshop. /// CONTENTS: royalty-free music featuring the sound and feel of the 50's, 60's and 70's. /// DOWNLOAD: free sample Mp3. /// AWARDS: American Design Awards (rating: 90 = platinum), Internet Tiny Awards (featured site). /// COST: 6 weeks.

FOO FIGHTERS
www.foofighters.com

USA
2005

Highlights

Amazingly illustrated but fast-paced website, with content from Tour to Community, from Shop to Music. /// Site incroyablement illustré mais néanmoins rapide, avec des contenus de toutes sortes : Tournées, Fan club, Boutique, Musique, etc. /// Erstaunlich illustrierte aber schnell reagierende Website, die Inhalte von Tour bis Fangemeinde und von Shop bis Musik bietet.

Info

DESIGN: Bukwild <www.bukwild.com>. /// PROGRAMMING: Jeff Toll & Dusty Brown & Robert Reinhard <www.bukwild.com>. /// TOOLS: CMS, PHP, Adobe Photoshop, Macromedia Flash, Adobe Illustrator. /// CONTENTS: home, news, press, bios, timeline, dictionary, FAQ, audio, video, photos, extras, discography, songlist, tabs, current tour, black box, messageboard, links, causes, buy. /// DOWNLOAD: Mp3 player, wallpapers, screensavers, ecard. /// AWARDS: e-creative.net, moluv.com. /// COST: 100 hours.

FORT MINOR

www.fortminor.com

Highlights Exceptional use of 3D effects in flash, all dynamic content becomes part of the artistic design, high quality audio in audio player. /// Utilisation exceptionnelle des effets 3D en Flash ; tous les contenus dynamiques participent du design artistique ; très bonne qualité audio du lecteur. /// Ungewöhnlicher Einsatz von 3D-Effekten in Flash. Die dynamischen Inhalte werden Teil des künstlerischen Designs. Hohe Audio-Qualität des Audio-Players.

Info DESIGN AND PROGRAMMING: Sparkart LLC. /// TOOLS: Adobe Photoshop, Macromedia Flash, CMS, xhtml. /// CONTENTS: band info, tourdates, photos, message board. /// DOWNLOAD: audio, video, screensavers, wallpapers. /// COST: 1 month.

FRED PERRY SUBCULTURE

www.fredperry.com/subculture

Highlights

Subculture is unique in that it brings the cream of new British musical talent to a worldwide audience, alongside artists from the Heritage of the Fred Perry brand such as Paul Weller. /// Subculture est unique en ce qu'il fait connaître la crème des nouveaux talents musicaux britanniques à une audience internationale, mais également des artistes appartenant à la lignée de la marque Fred Perry tel que Paul Weller. /// Subculture ist einzigartig, da sie die besten neuen britschen Talente vor ein weltweites Publikum bringt, darunter Künstler wie Paul Weller.

Info

DESIGN: De Facto <www.de-facto.com>. /// PROGRAMMING: Tom Stimpson, James Down <www.de-facto.com>. /// TOOLS: Macromedia Flash, xhtml, CMS, Adobe Photoshop, Macromedia Freehand, ASP. /// CONTENTS: band sections, reviews, sample tracks, competitions, video clips, tips on bands to watch out for. /// DOWNLOAD: downloadable tracks, screensavers, music player. /// COST: 240 hours.

FUR PATROL

www.furpatrol.com

NEW ZEALAND
2005

Highlights

Custom Flash CMS system allowing user to upload photos, mp3s, news & live gigs. Rich illustrative visuals. Sliding folder navigation. /// Système CMS Flash personnalisé permettant à l'utilisateur de télécharger vers le site des photos, des fichiers mp3, des news & concerts live. Visuels richement illustrés. Navigation par menus coulissants. /// Anwendungsspezifisches Flash CMS System ermöglicht dem Besucher den Upload von Fotos, MP3s, sowie News & Live Gigs. Reichlich Bildmaterial. Sliding-Folder-Navigation.

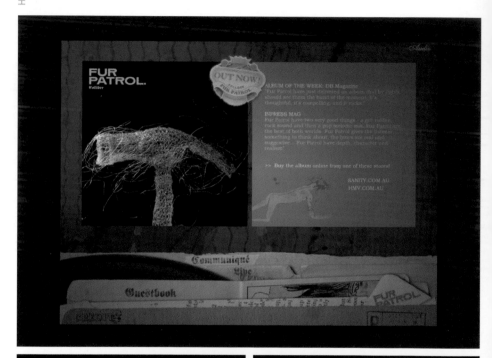

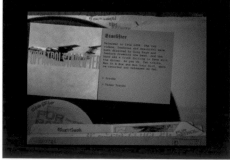

Info

DESIGN: RESN <www.resn.co.nz>. /// TOOLS: Adobe Photoshop, Macromedia Flash, PHP, CMS. /// CONTENTS: video clips, photos, music. /// AWARDS: TINY, 4efx, plasticpilots, kingforaweek.com. /// COST: 3 months.

FORD FUSION MIXER

http://fusionmixer.fordvehicles.com

Highlights

Each genre is broken down into Rhythm, Harmony, Melody, Lead, and Arrangement channels, each becoming 1 channel of the 5 channel mixer - making every mix unique. /// Chaque genre est décomposé en plusieurs canaux : rythme, harmonie, mélodie, instrument principal et arrangements, chacun devenant l'un des 5 canaux de mixage - chaque mix est ainsi absolument unique. /// Jedes Genre wird in Kanäle für Rhythmus, Harmonie, Melodie, Lead und Arrangement aufgeteilt, wobei jedes einen Kanal im 5-Kanal-Mixer darstellt. Dadurch wir jeder Mix einzigartig.

Info

DESIGN AND PROGRAMMING: AgencyNet <www.agencynet.com>. /// TOOLS: XML, CMS, SQL, .NET, Adobe Photoshop, Marromedia Flash.

GEORGE HARRISON

www.georgeharrison.com

Highlights The look and feel of the site plays off George's love for nature and spirituality, particularly his fondness for the lotus blossom. Content is easily editable by the client via CMS. /// L'allure du site et ce qu'il transmet traduisent l'amour et l'intérêt de Georges pour la nature et la spiritualité, et plus particulièrement son goût pour la fleur de lotus. Le contenu est facilement éditable par le client via CMS. /// Das Aussehen und die Atmosphäre der Website zeigt George's Liebe zur Natur und Spiritualität, besonders seine Vorliebe für Lotusblüten. Durch CMS-Technik ist der Inhalt vom Besucher leicht zu bearbeiten.

Info DESIGN AND PROGRAMMING: KNI <www.kurtnoble.com>. /// TOOLS: Adobe Photoshop, Adobe Illustrator, Macromedia Flash, PHP, CMS. /// CONTENTS: news, photo gallery, store, videos, complete discography, message board. /// DOWNLOAD: audio, video, wallpapers, photos. /// AWARDS: FWA. /// COST: 275 hours.

GLIDEASCOPE
www.glideascope.com

UK
2005

Highlights Interesting navigation concept, a very simplistic but overall atmospheric website. /// Concept de navigation intéressant, site Web très simple, mais atmosphère d'ensemble assez réussie. /// Interessantes Navigationskonzept, sehr simplistische aber schöne und atmosphärische Website.

Info DESIGN AND PROGRAMMING: 247 Media Studios <www.24-7media.de>. /// TOOLS: Adobe Photoshop, Adobe After Effects, Macromedia Flash, Cinema 4D. /// CONTENTS: music, photos, text. /// COST: 2 weeks.

MUSIC SITES • 107

GREAT MUSIC SHOP

www.greatmusicshop.com

Highlights GreatMusicShop is one of our own companies where we sell cool loops for cool sites. There are close to 50 music loops of different styles ranging in price from $29-$49. /// GreatMusicShop est l'une des sociétés où nous vendons des boucles 'cools' pour les sites 'cools'. On y trouve une cinquantaine de loops musicaux de différents styles, pour des prix échelonnés entre 29 et 49 dollars. /// GreatMusicShop ist eine unserer eigenen Firmen, über die wir coole Loops für coole Seiten vertreiben. Wir können nahezu 50 Loops verschiedener Musikstile anbieten, die sich preislich zwischen $29 und $49 bewegen.

Info DESIGN AND PROGRAMMING: GreatExposures <www.greatexposures.com>. /// TOOLS: Macromedia Flash, Adobe Photoshop, Adobe Audition, PHP, XHTML, Actionscript, XML. /// CONTENTS: music loops, text. /// COST: $7,000.

GREEDY WHITE CITIZENS

www.gwcmusic.com

Highlights

To reflect the tone & heart of the music the site was designed using real photographic elements. Textures that were worn in and had been through a life of their own produce a look that gives it its own character. /// Pour refléter le ton et le cœur de la musique, le site a été construit à partir d'éléments photographiques réels. Les textures y ont acquis une vie indépendante qui se traduit par un look unique en son genre. /// Um Ton und Herz der Musik zu reflektieren, wurde die Website aus realen Fotoelementen kreiert. Gewebe und Strukturen, die schon einiges hinter sich haben, schaffen eine Ansicht mit eigenem Charakter.

Info

DESIGN: Wiretree <www.wiretree.com>. /// **PROGRAMMING:** Will Weyer <www.wiretree.com>, <www.freshpixels.com>. /// **TOOLS:** Adobe Adobe Photoshop, Adobe Illustrator, Macromedia Flash, Macromedia Dreamweaver, Sorenson Squeeze. /// **CONTENTS:** photos, music video, video footage of live shows, tour shedule, animation, lyrics, bios. /// **DOWNLOAD:** custom music player (featuring full-length tracks), wallpapers, icons. /// **COST:** 185 hours.

HEADBANGERS.TV

www.headbangers.tv

The whole drawing of the city was made in one hour. It has been filmed and you can see it in the video section, named "making of". /// *Le dessin de la ville a été exécuté d'un seul jet en une heure. L'opération a été filmée et on peut la voir à la section vidéo, sous l'intitulé "making of".* /// Der erste Entwurf der gesamten Stadt wurde innerhalb einer Stunde fertiggestellt. Sie wurde gefilmt und ist im Videoteil unter "making of" zu sehen.

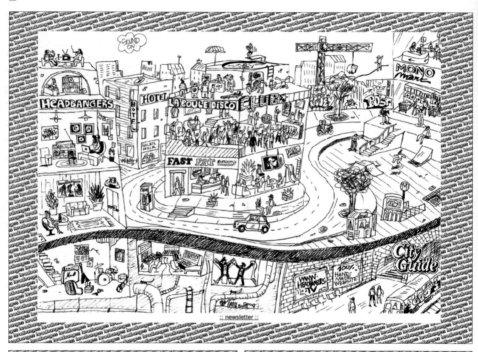

DESIGN: SO-ME <so-me.eu>. /// PROGRAMMING: Soleil Noir <www.soleilnoir.com>. /// TOOLS: all hand drawned on paper, then scanned, and programmed with Macromedia Flash. /// CONTENTS: informational site about Pedro Winter's artist management agency (daft punk, DJ Mehdi ...). /// COST: a few weeks for the programming, but one day for the whole drawing.

HEFTY RECORDS

www.heftyrecords.com

Highlights

The graphic design of the site is determined dynamically by the number of titles currently in the library. Integrated audio player. Based shopping cart and store. /// Le design graphique du site est dynamiquement déterminé par le nombre de titres actuellement en bibliothèque. Lecteur audio intégré. Boutique et panier d'achats. /// Das Grafikdesign der Site ist dynamisch bestimmt durch die aktuelle Anzahl der Titel in der Sammlung. Integrierter Audio-Player. Einkaufswagen und Shop.

Info

DESIGN AND PROGRAMMING: TENDER Creative LLC <www.tendercreative.com>. /// **TOOLS:** PHP, MySQL, Macromedia Flash, XML. /// **CONTENTS:** audio files, artist profiles, tour listings, discographies, shopping cart & store unit, photos, videos, downloads. /// **DOWNLOAD:** Mp3, wallpapers, photos, AIM icons.

HERBIE HANCOCK

www.herbiehancock.com

Highlights

Herbiehancock.com features an interactive, animated timeline with video and audio elements, giving users an entertaining way to quickly browse through the milestones of Herbie's career. /// Herbiehancock.com comprend un parcours chronologique animé interactif, avec des éléments audio et vidéo, offrant au visiteur une amusante façon de se balader au gré des grandes dates de la carrière du pianiste. /// Herbiehancock.com bietet eine interaktive und animierte Zeitleiste mit Video- und Audio-Elementen, die dem Besucher unterhaltsam ermöglicht, schnell durch die Meilensteine von Herbie's Karriere zu browsen.

Info

DESIGN: Erick Laubach, Tracey Bolton (Cottonblend) <www.cottonblend.com>. /// PROGRAMMING: Richard Tafoya (Cottonblend). /// FLASH PROGRAMMING: Sandra Eddy (Cottonblend). /// TOOLS: Adobe Photoshop, Adobe Illustrator, Macromedia Flash, Macromedia Fireworks, Custom Database-Driven CMS, PHP/MySql, XHTML. /// CONTENTS: Photos (family, personal, tour). Videos (interviews, performances, the 'making of'). Tour (past tours, current tours). Audio clips (highlights from the latest album). Flash Animation (significant life milestones). Biography. /// DOWNLOAD: Press kit. /// COST: 240 hours.

HIGHER FREQUENCY

www.higher-frequency.com

Highlights

Japan's Biggest Online-Multimedia site for Serious Dance Music. /// Le plus grand site multimédia japonais on-line, pour les amateurs de dance authentique. /// Japan's größte Online-Multimedia-Show für richtige Dance Music.

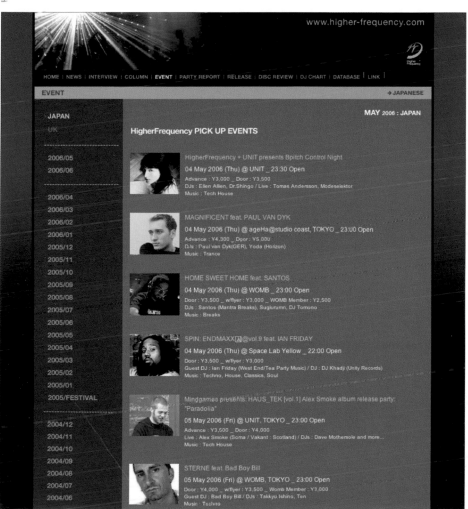

Info

DESIGN: artless Inc <www.artless.gr.jp>. /// **PROGRAMMING:** Masashi Kitagawa. /// **TOOLS:** Adobe Softwares, Macromedia Flash. /// **CONTENTS:** club music news, DJ interviews text and video, disc reviews, party reports, DJ charts and event information.

HOPE PARTLOW

www.hopepartlow.com

Highlights

Hope Partlow is a young singer whose music is based on her personal diary. The effect gives users an inside look into Hope's lyrics and the stories that inspire them. /// Hope Partlow est une jeune chanteuse qui tire sa musique de son journal intime. L'utilisateur a ainsi le sentiment de pénétrer l'intimité des textes de Hope, et des histoires qui les lui ont inspirés. /// Hope Partlow ist eine junge Sängerin, deren Musik auf ihrem persönlichen Tagebuch basiert. Der Effekt gibt Besuchern einen Einblick in Hope's Texte und die Geschichten, die sie inspirierten.

Info

DESIGN AND PROGRAMMING: Fahrenheit Studio <www.fahrenheit.com>. /// **TOOLS:** Macromedia Flash, Adobe Photoshop, Adobe Illustrator, CMS, HTML. /// **CONTENTS:** photos, audio/video, tour, bio, journal, animation, message board. /// **DOWNLOAD:** photos, wallpapers, buddy icons. /// **COST:** 100 hours.

Japan's First Ever Digital Dance Music Shop with Thousands of Great Club Tunes. /// Première boutique japonaise en ligne de digital dance, avec des milliers de grands titres. /// Japan's erster digitaler Dance-Music Shop mit tausenden großartigen Club Titeln.

Info

DESIGN: artless Inc. <www.artless.gr.jp>. /// PROGRAMMING: Kenij Kabashima and Shoshun Saeki [Black Bath] <www.black-bath.com>. /// TOOLS: Ajax, CMS, Adobe Softwares, Macromedia Flash. /// CONTENTS: Mp3 Data, shopping page [t-shirts, DJ gear, DTM software]. /// DOWNLOAD: Mp3.

IMAGINE MUSIC STORE

www.imaginemusicstore.com

Highlights

Original concept, Flash loading times and 100% dynamic. /// Conception originale, temps de chargement en Flash ; 100% dynamique. /// Originales Konzept, Flash-Ladezeiten und 100% dynamisch.

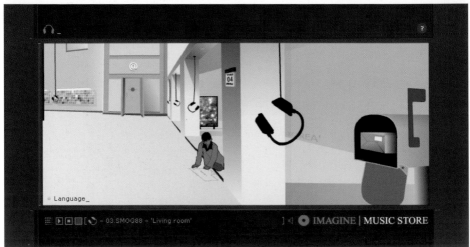

Info

DESIGN: xy area <www.xyarea.com>. /// PROGRAMMING: Fx. Marciat, J. Veronesi, P. Charlier (store) <www.xyarea.com>. /// TOOLS: Macromedia Flash, HTML, yaddmax CMS, PHP, XML, MySql, Macromedia Fireworks. /// CONTENTS: online store, CD, DVD, Mp3, photos, news, games. /// DOWNLOAD: samples, wallpapers, screensavers. /// AWARDS: Coolest Designs, PixelMakers. /// COST: 2 months.

IMUSIC NETWORK

www.i-musicnetwork.com

Highlights

Slick animations, a 3D layout and the use of rich wooden textures were employed to create a unique and very emotional browsing experience. /// Des animations astucieuses, une maquette en 3D et le recours aux riches textures du bois concourent à assurer au visiteur une expérience de navigation très intense. /// Gute Animationen, ein 3D-Layout und die Verwendung von satten Holzstrukturen wurden aufgenommen, um ein einzigartiges und sehr emotionales Browse-Erlebnis zu schaffen.

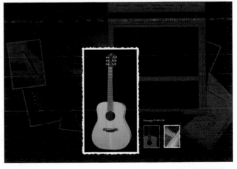

Info

DESIGN AND PROGRAMMING: Filigrafix Media Design <www.filigrafix.de>. /// TOOLS: Macromedia Flash, Macromedia Fireworks, Adobe Photoshop, Adobe Illustrator. /// CONTENTS: animated online catalogue of acoustic guitars. /// COST: 2 months.

THE CONCRETES IN-COLOUR

UK
2006

www.in-colour.net

Find secret downloadable content, including mobile content and PSP downloads. Create your own Concretes inspired artwork, save it to the website and send it to your friends. /// Débusquez des contenus téléchargeables, y compris pour portable et PSP. Créer votre propre maquette inspirée des Concretes, enregistrez-la sur le site et envoyez-la à vos amis. /// Geheimnisvolle Inhalte stehen zum Download zur Verfügung, einschließlich Mobil-Inhalte und PSP-Download. Der Besucher kann sein eigenes, von Concretes inspiriertes Kunstwerk schaffen, es auf der Website speichern und an Freunde versenden.

Highlights

www.theconcretes.com

made by **Bloc**

Info

DESIGN: John Denton (Bloc Media) <www.blocmedia.com>. /// **PROGRAMMING:** Xavier Monvoisin, Iain Lobb (Bloc Media). /// **TOOLS:** Macromedia Flash (with Actionscript 2), html, php, MySQL (running under Apache). /// **CONTENTS:** animations, audio samples, user generated artwork. /// **DOWNLOAD:** audio samples, desktops, mobile assets, PSP downloads. /// **AWARDS:** FWA (Site of the Day). /// **COST:** 2 weeks.

J'AIME NATASHA

www.jaimenatasha.ca

Highlights

Easily and entirely skinnable. All dynamic contents. A frenchy rock'n'roll delight. /// Aisément et entièrement 'skinnable'. Tous les contenus sont dynamiques. Un petit délice de rock'n'roll à la française. /// Einfach und schematisch änderbar. Alle Inhalte sind dynamisch aufgebaut. Ein französisches Rock'n'roll-Vergnügen.

Info

DESIGN AND PROGRAMMING: Mecano <www.mecano.ca>. /// TOOLS: Adobe Photoshop, Macromedia Flash, CSS. /// CONTENTS: photo, Mp3, blog. /// DOWNLOAD: press kit.

JJ APPLETON

USA
2005

www.jjappleton.com

Highlights

Multi-track, audio player. Video/image gallery. Downloads: mp3's, Aim icons & wallpaper. /// Lecteur audio multipistes. Galerie vidéo et images. A télécharger : fichiers mp3, icônes Aim et fonds d'écran. /// Multitrack, Audio Player. Video/Bild-Gallerie. Downloads: MP3's, Aim Icons & Hintergrund.

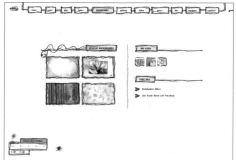
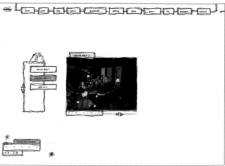

Info

DESIGN: Edge Lab Inc. <www.edgelabinc.com>. /// PROGRAMMING: Alon Zouratz <www.under-constructions.info>. /// TOOLS: Macromedia Flash, Macromedia Freehand, PHP, Sorenson Squeeze, Adobe Photoshop. /// CONTENTS: Mp3, video-clips, images, lyrics. /// DOWNLOAD: AIM icons, wallpapers, Mp3. /// AWARDS: Pixelmakers, Graphic Orgasm, highfloater, kingforaweek. /// COST: 120 hours.

JOTA QUEST

www.jotaquest.com.br

Band profile and band member's personal information with performance video highlights. The site's music player features all of the band's songs, organized by album. /// Profil du groupe, infos personnelles sur ses membres et best of de ses performances vidéo. Le lecteur de musique du site comprend toutes les chansons du groupe, organisées par album. /// Bandprofil und persönliche Informationen zu den Bandmitgliedern mit Performance-Video. Der Musik-Player der Website spielt alle Songs der Band, die nach Alben geordnet sind.

DESIGN: Bruno Fraga (6D Estúdio) <www.6d.com.br>. /// PROGRAMMING: Marlus (6D Estúdio). /// TOOLS: php, Adobe Photoshop, Adobe Illustrator, Adobe After Effects, Macromedia Flash. /// CONTENTS: photo, video-clips, tour, animation, press area, radio. /// DOWNLOAD: wallpapers, photos, release, logos, technical specifications for shows. /// COST: 6 weeks.

JULIET

www.julietsounds.com

Juliet's unique sound is a rich mixture of pop, electronica and dance. Using both organic and digital elements, we created an elaborate animated texturescape to complement the layered sound. /// Le son unique de Juliet est un riche mélange de pop, d'électronique et de dance. En recourant aux éléments organiques et numériques, nous avons créé un complexe paysage de textures animées pour compléter la maquette sonore. /// Juliet's einzigartiger Sound ist eine satte Mischung aus Pop, Electronica und Dance. Unter Verwendung von organischen und digitalen Elementen, kreierten wir eine raffiniert animierte Texturlandschaf, um den geschichteten Sound zu komplementieren.

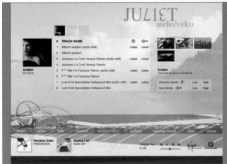

DESIGN AND PROGRAMMING: Fahrenheit Studio <www.fahrenheit.com>. /// **TOOLS:** Macromedia Flash, Adobe Photoshop, Adobe Illustrator, CMS, HTML. /// **CONTENTS:** photos, audio/video, tour, bio, journal, animation, message board. /// **DOWNLOAD:** photos, wallpapers, buddy icons. /// **AWARDS:** Creativity Award, Horizon Interactive Award. /// **COST:** 100 hours.

JUNIOR SENIOR

www.juniorsenior.com

Highlights

This site has so many hidden gems that it makes Legend of Zelda seem like Atari Adventure <www.warrenrobinett.com/adventure>. /// Ce site renferme tellement de joyaux cachés qu'à ses côtés la Légende de Zelda ressemble à au jeu Atari <www.warrenrobinett.com/adventure>. /// Diese Website bietet so viele versteckte Juwelen, dass sie Legend of Zelda wie ein Atari-Abenteuer aussehen läßt. <www.warrenrobinett.com/adventure>.

Info

DESIGN: Raz (Diet Strychnine Corp.) <www.dietstrychnine.com>. /// PROGRAMMING: Rasmus Blaesbjerg <www.woerk.com>. /// TOOLS: Adobe Photoshop, Adobe Illustrator, DHTML. /// CONTENTS: everything you could imagine. Easter eggs galore. /// DOWNLOAD: samples, tracks, Mp3, wallpapers, screensavers, photos. /// AWARDS: Nominated for MTV Europe Music Award 2003. /// COST: 200 hours of craziness!

KORN

USA

http://korn.sparkart.com

2004

Highlights: All original illustration work done in-house, seven individual characters are randomized, character with Korn beanie is a fan who won a contest to be integrated into the site. /// Une originale illustration du travail fait par la maison ; sept personnages individuels sont randomisés, celui qui porte le bonnet 'Korn beanie' est un fan ayant remporté un concours dont le prix était une apparition sur le site. /// **Alle Illustrationen wurden intern entworfen. Sieben individuelle Figuren wurden willkürlich ausgewählt. Die Figur mit Korn-Mütze ist ein Fan, der in einem Wettbewerb gewonnen hatte, in der Site integriert zu sein.**

DESIGN AND PROGRAMMING: Sparkart LLC. /// **TOOLS:** Adobe Illustrator, Adobe Photoshop, Macromedia Flash, CMS, xhtml. /// **CONTENTS:** band info, tour dates, photos, message board. /// **DOWNLOAD:** audio, video, screensavers, wallpapers. /// **COST:** 2 months.

Highlights

Listen to samples from the limited edition Kraftwerk album, 'Minimum - Maximum'. Create your own A/V show by overlaying animations to the live action video footage. /// Écoutez les samplers de l'édition limitée de l'album de Kraftwerk 'Minimum - Maximum'. Créez votre propre show A/V en superposant des animations au métrage vidéo en live. /// Samples von der limitierten Auflage des Kraftwerk-Albums 'Minimum - Maximum'. Bastel deine eigene Audio/Video-Show, indem du Animationen über Live-Videos legst.

Info

DESIGN: Liam Owen (Bloc Media) <www.blocmedia.com>. /// PROGRAMMING: Iain Lobb (Bloc Media). /// TOOLS: Macromedia Flash (with Actionscript 2), html, php, MySQL (running under Apache). /// CONTENTS: animations, audio samples, video samples. /// DOWNLOAD: wallpapers, mobile assets. /// COST: 1 week.

KRAZY BALDHEAD

www.krazybaldhead.com

Highlights

Psychedelic animations based on record cover art (record cover by So Me). /// Animations psychédéliques basées sur l'illustration de couverture du disque (dont l'auteur est So Me). /// Psychedelische Animation basiert auf den Plattencover-Illustrationen (Plattencover von So Me).

Info

DESIGN: Emile Shahidi and drawings by So Me <www.arcademode.com>, <www.edbangerrecords.com>. /// PROGRAMMING: Emile Shahidi <www.arcademode.com>. /// TOOLS: Adobe Illustrator, Macromedia Flash, php, xml. /// CONTENTS: photos, videos, audio songs, news. /// COST: 10 days.

LAURA TURNER
www.lauraturnermusic.com

Highlights

Elegant scene transitions make the experience inviting and relaxing. A butterfly was incorporated to mark the navigation system and a simple wing animation is triggered by touch. /// D'élégantes scènes de transition rendent l'expérience séduisante et relaxante. Le papillon qui a été ajouté pour indiquer le navigateur bat des ailes lorsqu'on l'effleure. /// Elegante Szenenübergänge machen das Erlebnis der Site einladend und entspannend. Ein Schmetterling markiert das Navigationssystem und einfache Animationen werden durch Klicken ausgelöst.

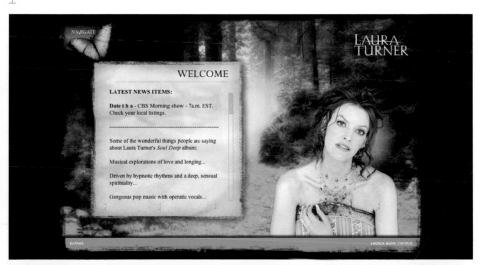

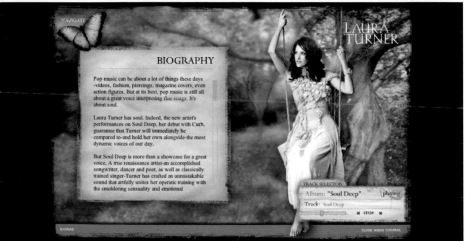

Info

DESIGN: Wiretree <www.wiretree.com>. /// PROGRAMMING: Scott Cook, Will Weyer, Jeff Askew (Wiretree). /// TOOLS: Adobe Photoshop, Adobe Illustrator, Adobe After Effects, Macromedia Flash, Macromedia Dreamweaver. /// CONTENTS: photos, music video, tour dates, animation, lyrics. /// DOWNLOAD: Mp3 samples, wallpapers. /// AWARDS: several web design site awards and link throughs. /// COST: 190 hours.

LESS THE BAND

http://lesstheband.com

The stop-motion animation technique as opposed to a vector or video simulation adds to the strength of the visuals. /// L'animation image par image opposée à la simulation en vecteur ou en vidéo renforce la puissance des visuels. /// Die Stop-Motion Animation trägt im Gegensatz zu einer Vektor- oder Video-Simulation zur Stärke der Bilder bei.

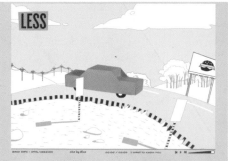

DESIGN AND PROGRAMMING: Also <www.also-online.com>. /// TOOLS: Adobe Photoshop, Adobe Illustrator, Macromedia Dreamweaver, Macromedia Flash. /// CONTENTS: photos, animation. /// DOWNLOAD: Mp3. /// AWARDS: FWA [Site of the Day]. /// COST: 300 hours.

LE TAXIPROD

FRANCE
2004

Beat synchronized Radio. Skinnable radio. Dynamic content. /// Radio synchronisée. Radio skinnable. Contenu dynamique. /// Beat-synchronisiertes Radio mit veränderbaren Oberflächen. Dynamischer Inhalt.

Highlights

NOW PLAYING :
Akka&Wounl : Blessed Dreams
SELECT PLAYLIST :

SELECT TRACK :
Akka&Wounl : Blessed Dreams
V2V : Dreaming Faction
Akka : Face the Fact
Red Hat : Warmentz : Break Da rule
Ma Crew : Continuum
Freecab : Establishing Contact
V2V : Call it Blues
Freecab : Taxi Gratuit 2

NEWS

2005
FREECAB in move

MORE NEWZ

EVENTS !

27/04/05
SANTA CREW 20

17/02/05
SANTA CREW [FEAT TERRY
-T (uk)]
AT NOUVEAU CASINO (Paris)

15/12/05
SANTA CREW 18

AT NOUVEAU CASINO (Paris)

MORE EVENTS

RELEASES

LTP 001 - RESET, A
FINE NU-JAZZ &
BREAKBEAT
SELECTION

MORE RELEASES

TAXI STUFFS

LAST DOWNLOAD
CODEK PARTY III AT
NOUVEAU CASINO

FILMS
PICTURES
OTHER STUFFS

LE TAXI PROD

▸ WHO ARE WE ?
▸ PRESS
▸ CONTACTS BOOKING
▸ SERVICES

ARTISTS

FREECAB
NU-JAZZ COMBO

VALSES 2 VIENNE
LIVE BREAKBEAT

santa crew
DRUMS, VIDEO & BASS

BBC SOUND SYSTEM
LIVE FROM SENEGAL

iDUB
ELECTRO DUB

the infamous
INOPERATIVE VISUAL ART

Pixelles
VJ'S ALL STARLETTES

REVERSE
BLACK & WHITE VEEJAY

N: Gallien Guibert <www.thegenre.com>. /// PROGRAMMING: Fabrice Depoix <www.clebar.com>. /// TOOLS: Macromedia Flash, XML, Flashamp. /// TS: video, photo, animations, sounds. /// DOWNLOAD: Press kit, Flyers. /// COST: 100 hours.

LINKIN PARK

www.linkinpark.com

Highlights

Uses art from Breaking The Habit video and live photos, regularly updated video content in LP Newscaster, high quality audio in audio player. /// Utilise des vidéos et des photos en live de Breaking The Habit ; contenu des actualités LP régulièrement actualisé ; son du lecteur audio de grande qualité. /// Verwendet Kunst vom Breaking The Habit-Video und Live-Fotos, regelmäßig aktualisierter Videoinhalt im LP Newscaster, hohe Qualität der Audio-Elemente.

Info

DESIGN AND PROGRAMMING: Sparkart LLC. /// TOOLS: Adobe Photoshop, Macromedia Flash, CMS, xhtml. /// CONTENTS: band info, tourdates, photos, ᵐ board. /// DOWNLOAD: audio, video, screensavers, wallpapers. /// COST: 2 months.

LLOYD LANDESMAN

USA
2005

www.lloydlandesman.com

Highlights

Animated equalizer. Full customer login platform. Full video/sound gallery. /// Égalisateur animé. Plateforme de connexion client complète. Galerie son et vidéo complète. /// Animierter Equalizer. Ausgedehnte Login-Plattform. Große Video/Sound-Gallerie.

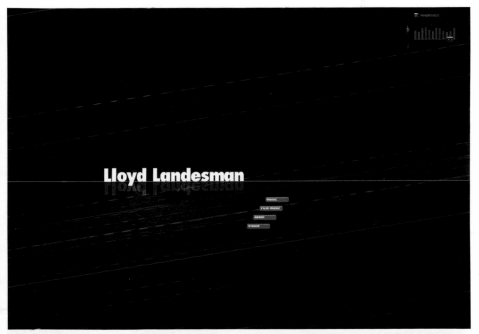

Info

DESIGN: Edge Lab Inc. <www.edgelabinc.com>. /// PROGRAMMING: Alon Zourtetz <www.under-constructions.info>. /// TOOLS: Macromedia Flash, Macromedia Freehand, php, MySUL, FlashAmpPro, Sorenson Squeeze, Adobe Photoshop. /// CONTENTS: Mp3, video-clips, dynamic equalizer. /// AWARDS: TINY, DOPE, fcukstar, kingforaweek, pixelmakers. /// COST: 160 hours.

LONTRA MUSIC

www.lontramusic.com

Highlights

The black and white look of the site contrasts with the surprise behind each speaker box. This website brings all information about the studio to you in a very funny environment. /// Le look noir et blanc du site contraste avec la surprise cachée derrière chaque haut-parleur. On trouve sur ce site toutes sortes d'infos au sujet du studio, dans un environnement très fun. /// Das schwarzweiße Aussehen der Website kontrastiert mit der Überraschung, die hinter jedem Lautsprecher steckt. Diese Site bietet alle Informationen über das Studio in einer sehr lustigen Umgebung.

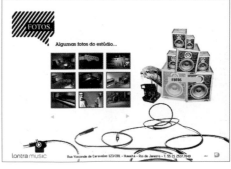

Info

DESIGN AND PROGRAMMING: Dimaquina <www.dimaquina.com>. /// TOOLS: php, Adobe Photoshop, Macromedia Flash, Macromedia Dreamweaver. /// CONTENTS: photo, video-clips, tour, animation. /// COST: 4 weeks.

LOOPLABS

www.looplabs.com

Highlights This was the premiere online mixing tool which has led to a multitude of further successful campaigns including Bacardi DJ. This site was featured by Steve Jobs of Apple at MacWorld 2003 when he first unveiled the Apple Safari browser. /// Cet outil de mixage on-line, le premier de tous, a été suivi de beaucoup d'autres campagnes réussies, dont celle de Bacardi DJ. Au Mac World 2003, ce site a été mis en vedette par Steve Jobs d'Apple, lorsqu'il a dévoilé le navigateur Apple Safari. /// Die Website bot das erste online-Mixing an, was zu vielen anderen erfolgreichen Kampagnen führte, unter anderem Bacardi DJ. Diese Site wurde von Steve Jobs of Apple bei MacWorld 2003 vorgestellt, als er zum ersten Mal den Apple Safari Browser bekannt machte.

Info DESIGN AND PROGRAMMING: CRASH!MEDIA <www.crashmedia.com>. /// TOOLS: Macromedia Flash, Adobe Photoshop. /// CONTENTS: sound samples and loops. /// AWARDS: Webby Award, SxSw Award, Flash Forward Film Festival, FITC Festival. /// COST: 1000 hours.

L'OREILLE

www.loreille.com

Highlights

Cool and clean design and a good example of how to integrate good flash animation, imagery and sound for storytelling. /// Conception cool et soignée, et bon exemple de comment intégrer une animation flash réussie, du son et des images pour raconter une histoire. /// Cooles und sauberes Design. Ein schönes Beispiel dafür, wie gute Flash-Animationen, Bilder und Sound in das Thema integriert werden können.

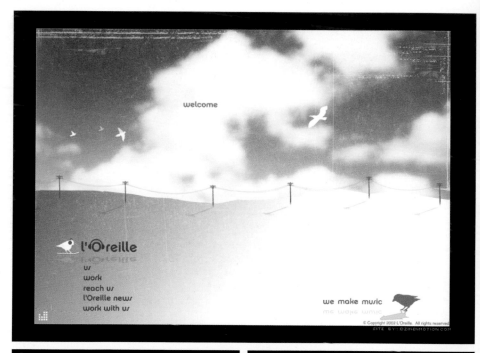

Info

DESIGN: Rose Pietrovito (dZinenmOtion) <www.dzinenmotion.com>. /// TOOLS: Adobe Photoshop, Macromedia Flash. /// CONTENTS: video and Mp3 clips. /// DOWNLOAD: Mp3. /// AWARDS: Cannes Lions (Gold), CLIO (Gold: Artistic Techniques and Self-Promotion), Digital Craft Musuem (Frankfurt, Germany), Marketing Awards - Gold (Toronto, Canada), Macromedia (Site of the Day).

LOWERCASE PEOPLE

www.lowercasepeople.com

lowercase people.com is an online magazine for artists in action. We are an interactive online magazine discussing rising artists and social justice issues not mentioned in mainstream media. /// lowercase people.com est une revue on-line pour artistes engagés. Nous sommes un magazine on-line interactif qui se fait l'écho des débats artistiques actuels et des questions de justice sociale dont ne parlent pas les mass médias. /// lowercase people.com ist ein Online-Magazin für Künstler in Aktion. Wir sind ein interaktives Online-Magazin, das über aufsteigende Künstler berichtet sowie über Fälle von sozialer Gerechtigkeit, die nicht in den generellen Medien erwähnt werden.

Highlights

Info **DESIGN:** Clark Studios <www.clark-studios.com>. /// **PROGRAMMING:** Ricky Truth <www.the-white-list.com>. /// **TOOLS:** PHP, MySql, Macromedia Flash, HTML, CSS. /// **CONTENTS:** photo, video-clips, reviews, music, articles, bulletin board. /// **DOWNLOAD:** Mp3, wallpapers, photos. /// **COST:** 100 hours.

LUCKY VOICE

www.luckyvoice.co.uk

Highlights

Lucky Voice is a new concept mixing karaoke with the look and feel of a stylish members' club. The site needed to develop on this to help build awareness and understanding as well as generate bookings. /// Lucky Voice est un nouveau concept, une espèce d'hybride entre karaoké et club privé classieux. Le site devait donc être construit sur cette base afin de contribuer à faire connaître le club et d'y multiplier les réservations. /// Lucky Voice ist ein neues Konzept: eine Mischung von Karaoke mit dem Aussehen und Gefühl eines stilvollen Clubs. Die Website wurde kreiert, um Bewusstsein und Verständnis zu schaffen sowie die Buchungen zu fördern.

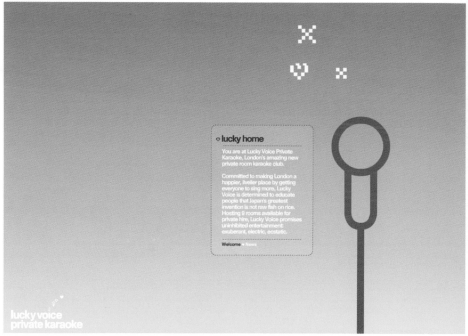

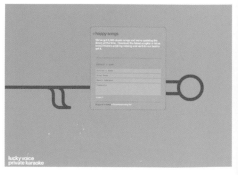

Info

DESIGN AND PROGRAMMING: de-construct <www.de-construct.com>. /// TOOLS: Adobe Photoshop, Macromedia Flash. /// CONTENTS: photos, editorial, animation. /// COST: 4 weeks.

THE MAGIC NUMBERS POSTER WALL

http://magic.blocmedia.net

2006

Highlights Sample the new single from The Magic Numbers. Create custom Magic Numbers artwork to send to your friends or download to your phone. ///
Découvrez le nouveau single de The Magic Numbers. Créez votre propre dessin Magic Numbers, et envoyez-le à vos amis ou téléchargez-le sur votre
portable. /// Die Website bietet Samples der neuen Single von The Magic Numbers sowie die Interaktion mit anderen Magic Numbers-Fans und die
Möglichkeit der Kreation eines Posters für die Notizenseite der Fangemeinde. Der Besucher kann spezifische Magic Numbers Kunstwerke
entwerfen und sie an seine Freunde senden oder auf sein Mobiltelefon laden.

Info DESIGN: Tom Jennings (Bloc Media) <www.blocmedia.com>. /// PROGRAMMING: Iain Lobb, Steve Hayes (Bloc Media). /// TOOLS: Macromedia Flash (with
Actionscript 2), html, php, MySQL (running under Apache). /// CONTENTS: audio samples, user generated artwork. /// DOWNLOAD: wallpapers, mobile
desktops. /// AWARDS: (Best Entertainment) Interactive Marketing and Advertising Award 2005, (Best Microsite) BIMAs 2005. /// COST: 1 week.

MUSIC SITES • 137

Highlights

Design, interface, transition. /// Design, interface, transition. /// Design, Interface, Übergänge.

Info

DESIGN: Ricardo Bräutigam <www.brautigam.com.br>. /// **PROGRAMMING:** Henrique Kywal. /// **TOOLS:** Adobe Photoshop, Macromedia Flash. /// **CONTENTS:** photos, videos, bio, tour dates, Mp3, etc. /// **DOWNLOAD:** Press kit. /// **AWARDS:** nominee to best website award at MTV Video Music Brazil 2005. /// **COST:** 96 hours.

MARNI ANGEL

www.marniangel.com

Highlights

A provocative, high-energy flash animation intro, magazine like presentation with a music box and an angel symbolizing the contrast in the music and the artist herself. /// Une animation d'intro provocante et énergique, une présentation très magazine avec une boîte à musique et un ange symbolisant le contraste au sein de la musique et de l'artiste elle-même. /// Eine provokative, energiegeladene Flash-Animation in der Einführung. Magazin-artige Präsentation mit einer Musikbox und einem Engel, der den Kontrast der Musik und der Künstlerin selbst symbolisiert. Dieses Meisterwerk bietet insgesamt eine leichte Navigation und schnelles Upload der Video-Clips.

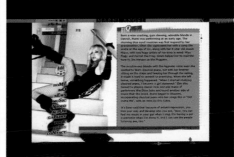

Info

DESIGN PROGRAMMING: GreatExposures <www.greatexposures.com>. /// TOOLS: Macromedia Flash, Adobe Photoshop, Adobe Premiere, Adobe Audition, Autodesk 3D Studio Max, PHP, XHTML, Actionscript, XML. /// CONTENTS: intro animation, photo gallery, video-clips. /// AWARDS: FWA (Site of the Day) 2005; ITA (Site of the Week) 2005; DOPE Award. /// COST: $10,000.

MERCEDES-BENZ MIXED TAPE GERMANY
www.mercedes-benz.de/mixedtape 2004

A fantastic example of how any industry can connect brands and customers using music and the Internet. The design is superb as well as the music. /// Un exemple fantastique de ce que peut faire l'industrie pour relier marques et consommateurs en utilisant la musique et Internet. Le design est superbe, de même que la musique. /// Ein fantastisches Beispiel dafür, wie jeder Industriezweig durch Musik und das Internet eine Handelsmarke mit ihren Kunden verbinden kann. Das Design ist hervorragend, genauso wie die Musik.

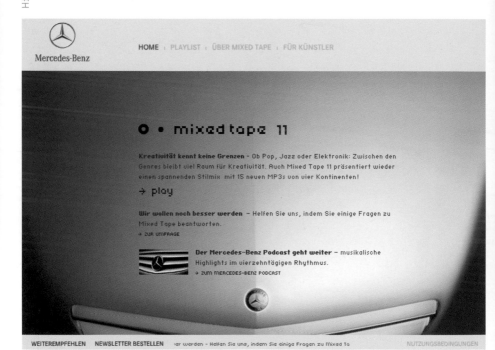

Info

DESIGN AND PROGRAMMING: Scholz & Volkmer GmbH <www.s-v.de>. /// TOOLS: MySQL, Delphi, Javascript, PHP, XML based, Macromedia Flash, HTML. /// CONTENTS: Every 10 weeks, a new compilation with about 15 songs is released. You can either listen to the pieces online, download them as a file or send them via ecard to friends. /// DOWNLOAD: music. /// AWARDS: Red Dot Communication Design Award, DDC-Award (Bronze), International Automotive Advertising Award (Silber), Cannes (Shortlist Cyber-Lion), New York Festivals Interactive (Silber).

MONOBLOCO

www.monobloco.com.br

Highlights

There is a tough but simple background administration system that allows for about 50% of the site's content to be user updatable. The band uses the site as a learning tool by posting learning material for the students to download. /// Un solide mais néanmoins simple système d'administration permet à l'utilisateur d'actualiser environ 50% des contenus. Le groupe utilise le site comme un outil d'apprentissage en y accrochant du matériel d'étude que les étudiants peuvent télécharger. /// Eine robustes, aber einfaches Verwaltungssystem sorgt dafür, dass ungefär 50% des Inhaltes der Site vom Besucher aktualisiert werden kann. Die Band benutzt die Website als Lern-Tool, indem sie Lernmaterial zum Download zur Verfügung stellt.

Info

DESIGN: Bê Vieira (6D Estúdio) <www.6d.com.br>. /// PROGRAMMING: Marlus (6D Estúdio). /// TOOLS: php, Adobe Photoshop, Adobe Illustrator, Adobe After Effects, Maya, Macromedia Flash. /// CONTENTS: photo, video-clips, tour, animation, press area, radio, student's area. /// DOWNLOAD: press photos, release, logos, technical specifications for concerts. /// COST: 8 weeks.

THE MOONSHINE PLAYBOYS

www.moonshineplayboys.com

This website shows the mood and the world of three ol' Blue Grass players who covers unexpected pop & rock songs "da blue grass way"! /// Ce site révèle l'humeur et le monde de trois musiciens de Blue Grass qui revisitent des chansons pop et rock assez inattendues, dans le bon vieux style d'autrefois! /// Diese Website zeigt die Stimmung und die Welt von drei alten Blue Grass-Spielern, die unerwartete Pop & Rock-Songs "the blue grass way" spielen!

DESIGN: Hypnotized Design <www.Hypnotized.org>. /// PROGRAMMING: Hypno Seven <www.Hypno7.com>. /// TOOLS: Adobe Photoshop, Macromedia Flash. /// CONTENTS: photos, animations, sound effects. /// DOWNLOAD: hi-res photos, logos, sound samples. /// AWARDS: NewWebPick, Ades Award, Plastic Pilot, Yellow Pimiento, Pixelmakers, Strangefruits. /// COST: 50-60 hours.

MTV

www.mtv.co.uk

Highlights

Each MTV site's identity is a direct reflection of the television broadcast output, naturally tailored to fit an on-screen medium. The site is an incredibly flexible, modular structure. /// L'identité de chaque site MTV est le reflet direct de la production télévisuelle de la chaîne, tout naturellement faite pour s'ajuster à un media sur écran. Le site a une structure incroyablement flexible et modulaire. /// Jede MTV Website-Identität ist eine unmittelbare Reflexion der Fernsehausstrahlung und auf den Bildschirm zugeschnitten. Die Website hat eine unglaublich flexible und modulare Struktur.

Info

DESIGN AND PROGRAMMING: Preloaded <www.preloaded.com>. /// TOOLS: CSS/XHTML, Adobe Photoshop, Macromedia Fireworks. /// CONTENTS: show and channel support material.

AOL TOP 11

http://music.aol.com/top11/main

Highlights

The show is exclusively recorded for the AOL Top 11 application. The application has a cue point system that can trigger special events such as host comments and animations, synced to video time stamps. /// Le show a été exclusivement enregistré pour l'application AOL Top 11. L'application dispose d'un système de point Cue capable de déclencher des événements spéciaux : commentaires par host et animations, synchronisés avec des estampilles vidéo temporelles. /// Die Show wurde ausschließlich für die AOL Top 11-Anwendung aufgenommen. Sie bietet ein Cue Point-System, das spezielle Abläufe wie Host-Comments und Animationen auslöst.

Info

DESIGN AND PROGRAMMING: Fantasy Interactive <www.fantasy-interactive.com>. /// TOOLS: Adobe Photoshop, Macromedia Flash. /// CONTENTS: hosted music video top list show, image gallery, polls, message board, e-commerce. /// AWARDS: FWA (Site of the Day).

AOL SESSIONS

http://music.aol.com/videos/sessions

Highlights

A rich media experience that delivers an exciting interactive music countdown. /// Une riche expérience médiatique qui offre un passionnant compte à rebours musical interactif. /// Ein volles Media-Erlebnis, das einen aufregenden interaktiven Musik-Countdown liefert.

Info

DESIGN AND PROGRAMMING: Fantasy Interactive <www.fantasy-interactive.com>. /// TOOLS: Adobe Photoshop, Macromedia Flash. /// CONTENTS: photos, videos, web 2.0. /// AWARDS: FWA.

MUSICAL ARCHITECT

USA
2006

www.musicalarchitect.com

1.] Vinyl digital MP3 jukebox. 2.] Floating instruments. 3.] User Interaction. /// 1.] Juke-box numérique vinyle MP3 . 2.] Floating instruments. 3.] Interaction avec l'utilisateur. /// 1.] Vinyl digitale MP3 Jukebox. 2.] Fließende Instrumente. 3.] Benutzer-Interaktion.

DESIGN: mocaFusion Media Group, Inc. <www.mocaFusion.com>. /// PROGRAMMING: Albert Lan <www.albertlan.com>. /// TOOLS: Macromedia Flash, Actionscript, Adobe Photoshop, Adobe Illustrator, XML, PHP, Javascript. /// CONTENTS: image gallery, tour, guestbook, animation, custom playlist. /// AWARDS: TINY (Site of the Week), Pixel Makers (Site of the Week). /// COST: 60 hours.

MAKE MY PEOPLE SING

www.mypeople.com/sing/index.html

2005

Highlights Users can cue any of ten little people, or the brand's mascot, remix the company's jingle into a unique song, send the song to their friends, or save it in an international jukebox for others to enjoy. /// Les utilisateurs peuvent solliciter un ou plusieurs des petits personnages (la mascotte de la marque) pour remixer le jingle de la société et en faire une chanson unique qu'ils enverront à leurs amis ou enregistreront dans un juke-box international à l'intention d'autres auditeurs. /// Der Besucher kann zehn kleinen Männchen, die Markenmaskottchen, aufrufen und damit das Jingle des Unternehmens zu einem einzigartigen Song zusammenmischen. Der Song kann dann zu Freunden gesendet werden, damit auch andere daran Spaß haben können.

Info DESIGN PROGRAMMING: Domani Studios <www.domanistudios.com>. /// TOOLS: Macromedia Flash. /// CONTENTS: dynamically-created electronic music.

MUSIC SITES · 147

NEWAY KARAOKE

www.newaykb.com

Highlights

An exciting page for a Karaoke in Hong Kong featuring everything available from the dinner Menu to Great music. Definitely a good example to follow. /// Une page séduisante pour un Karaoké de HongKong, avec à l'écran tout ce qui y est disponible, du menu à la musique. Un exemple à suivre, sans aucun doute. /// Eine aufregende Website für ein Karaoke in Hong Kong, das alles Verfügbare anbietet - vom Dinnermenu bis hin zu großer Musik. Mit Sicherheit ein gutes Beispiel, dem man folgen sollte.

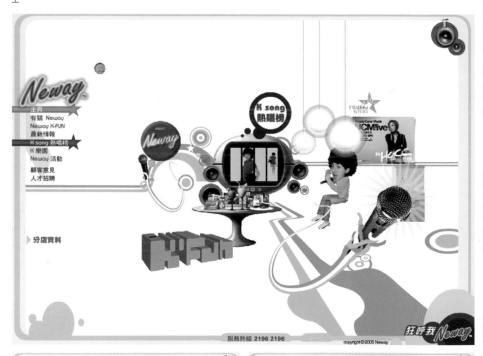

Info

DESIGN: Andrew Lee, Snowman Tsang, Kogi Ko, Sumato Li, Tom Shum [Rice 5] <www.rice5.com>. /// **PROGRAMMING:** Daniel Yuen, Eric Ho, Mike Li. /// **TOOLS:** xhtml, xml, php, Macromedia Firework, Macromedia Flash, Adobe Photoshop. /// **CONTENTS:** photo, video-clips, customize Ecrad, MTV, animation, games, promotional information, branch location map. /// **DOWNLOAD:** wallpapers, MSN icon. /// **AWARDS:** 2005 Interactive & Direct Awards [iDA] - Best Corporate Websites [Bronze]. /// **COST:** 300 hours.

NICK HALL

www.nick-hall.com

Highlights

Cool MP3 player developed with XML in order to make the tracklist easy to update. Metaphors using envelopes and pieces of paper to display the contents. Lots of contents and information. /// Lecteur MP3 sympa, développé avec XML de manière à pouvoir actualiser facilement la liste de morceaux. Des enveloppes et des bouts de papier sont utilisés comme supports pour afficher les contenus. Nombreux contenus et informations. /// Cooler MP3-Player, der mit XML entwickelt wurde, um einfache Updates der Track-Liste machen zu können. Auf Umschlägen und Papierblättern werden die Inhalte der Site gezeigt. Viele Inhalte und Infos.

Info

DESIGN: Emiliano Rodriguez <www.emilianorodriguez.com.ar>. /// PROGRAMMING: Emiliano Rodriguez and Nick Hall. /// TOOLS: Macromedia Flash, Macromedia Dreamweaver, Adobe Photoshop. /// CONTENTS: photos, Mp3. /// DOWNLOAD: wallpapers. /// AWARDS: Netdiver. /// COST: 90 hours.

NOVASTAR

www.novastar-music.com

Highlights

Exclusive Super 8 animation style. Full Flash media content. Text and media fully manageable. /// Animation en Super 8 exclusive. Contenu entièrement en Flash media. Texte et media entièrement administrables. /// Ausschließliche Super 8 Animation. Voller Flash-Media Inhalt. Texte und Media sind leicht zu handhaben.

Info

DESIGN: Antoine Menard, Alexandre Tyack (Soleil Noir) <www.soleilnoir.net>. /// **PROGRAMMING:** Maxime Montegnies (Soleil Noir). /// **PROJECT MANAGER:** Benjamin Laugel (Soleil Noir). /// **TOOLS:** Adobe Photoshop, Macromedia Flash, Adobe After Effects, XML, Php. /// **CONTENTS:** news, photo, video-clips, tour, biography. /// **COST:** 2 weeks.

OASIS
www.oasisinet.com

Highlights

for exclusive downloads; to chat with other fans, to keep informed on the band with the latest news/tour info; and listen to their favourite Oasis hits on Radio Supernova. /// Pour télécharger, chatter entre eux, tout connaître sur le groupe ou sa dernière tournée, écouter leurs thèmes préférés d'Oasis sur Radio Supernova. /// Für exklusive Downloads; um mit den anderen Fans zu chatten, um die neusten Infos über die Band und ihre Touren einzuholen; und um ihre Lieblingshits von Oasis über Radio Supernova zu hören.

Info

DESIGN: Prezence UK <www.prezence.co.uk>. /// TOOLS: Php, Mysql, xHTML, CMS, CSS, Javascript, XML, CMS, Adobe Photoshop, Macromedia Flash, Macromedia Dreamweaver. /// CONTENTS: news, audio samples, streaming 'Supernova' radio, photo galleries, fan submission galleries, video streams, full discography, gigography, reviews, lyrics, forum. /// DOWNLOAD: wallpapers. /// COST: 500 hours.

Highlights

Pete Philly's and perquisite's nice tunes. Wonderful photos. Smooth animations emphasize the music. /// Les beaux morceaux de Pete Philly's & Perquisite. Magnifiques photos. Une animation hyper souple met la musique en valeur. /// Pete Philly's schöne Melodien. Wundervolle Fotos. Weiche Animation unterstreicht die Musik.

Info

DESIGN AND PROGRAMMING: Huy Dieu (GOOQ) <www.gooq.de>. /// TOOLS: CMS, php, Adobe Photoshop, Macromedia Freehand, Macromedia Flash. /// CONTENTS: photo, tour, animation, streaming mp3, guestbook, gallery microsite. /// DOWNLOAD: music, video. /// COST: 20 days.

OZARK HENRY

www.ozarkhenry.com

Highlights

The site has a playful navigation with floating panels. All content is managed by means of a flash94 content management system: news, calendar, guest book, biography, discography, pictures... /// Navigation ingénieuse utilisant des panneaux flottants. Tous les contenus sont gérés par un système de gestion en flash94 : news, calendrier, registre d'invités, biographie, discographie, photos... /// Die Site bietet eine verspielte Navigation mit fließenden Elementen. Der gesamte Inhalt wird durch ein Flash94 Managementsystem gesteuert: News-Bereich, Kalender, Gästebuch, Biographie, Diskographie, Bilder...

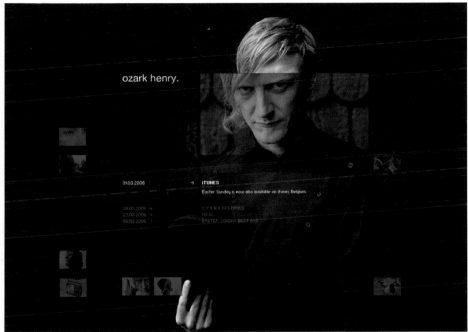

Info

DESIGN AND PROGRAMMING: group94 <www.group94.com>. /// TOOLS: Macromedia Freehand, Adobe Photoshop, Macromedia Flash. /// CONTENTS: news, calendar, video-clips, music, biography, guestbook. /// COST: 4 weeks.

PARAGON STUDIOS

www.paragon-studios.com

Highlights

Great background music, with smooth and fast navigation. Great design too. /// Excellent fond sonore, navigation souple et rapide. Le design est également remarquable. /// Großartige Hintergrundmusik sowie glatte und schnelle Navigation. Dazu kommt ein Klasse-Design.

Info

DESIGN: Wiretree <www.wiretree.com>. /// PROGRAMMING: Will Weyer, Scott Cook, Todd Anderson, Jeff Askew (Wiretree). /// TOOLS: Adobe Photoshop, Adobe Illustrator, Adobe After Effects, Macromedia Flash, Macromedia Dreamweaver. /// CONTENTS: photo tour, studio overview, services, list of gear, client list. /// DOWNLOAD: wallpapers, tracking diagram. /// AWARDS: several web design site awards and link throughs. /// COST: 290 hours.

PEACEFROG

www.peacefrog.com

2003

Getting to work with a label we'd loved since forever. /// Une première collaboration avec un label que nous aimons depuis toujours. /// Hier durften wir mit einer Marke arbeiten, die wir seit jeher liebten.

DESIGN AND PROGRAMMING: Kleber Design Ltd. <www.kleber.net>. /// TOOLS: Adobe Photoshop, Macromedia Flash, php, HTML, CMS. /// CONTENTS: label news, artist biographies, releases. /// COST: 4 months.

MUSIC SITES · 155

POLLINATION MUSIC

www.pollination-music.com

Highlights

Branding and site created together for original approach. Flash mp3 players integrated into pages. Designed for business and pleasure. /// Stratégie de marque et site ont été créés ensemble, pour une approche originale. Lecteur Flash mp3 intégré aux pages. Conçue pour le business et le plaisir. /// Marke und Website wurden zusammen für eine originäre Annäherung entwickelt. Die Seiten sind mit einem integrierten Flash MP3-Player ausgestattet. Die Website wurde für das Unternehmen und zum Vergnügen der Besucher entwickelt.

Info

DESIGN: Tim Dillon (Onscreen Creative) <www.onscreencreative.com>. /// PROGRAMMING: Rob Thomson <www.marotori.com>. /// TOOLS: Adobe Photoshop, Adobe illustrator, Macromedia Flash, PHP CMS. /// CONTENTS: artists info with Mp3 music players, writers biog's, company info. /// COST: 4 weeks.

PUMP AUDIO

www.pumpaudio.com

Highlights FastTrack: Pump Audio's artists can upload mp3s of their music to audition for Pump's catalog. Artist Wizard: Artists will be able to fill out Pump's license agreement via a dynamic Flash app. /// FastTrack : les artistes de Pump Audio peuvent télécharger vers le catalogue du site des fichiers mp3 de leur musique afin que le public puisse les écouter. Assistant de l'artiste : les artistes pourront remplir un accord de licence Pump par le biais d'une application Flash dynamique. /// FastTrack: Pump Audio's Künstler können MP3-Dateien mit ihrer Musik hochladen und im Pump-Katalog vorstellen. Artist Wizard: Die Künstler bekommen die Möglichkeit, Pump's Lizenzvereinbarung über eine dynamische Flash-Anwendung auszufüllen.

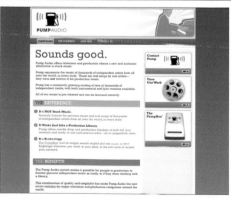

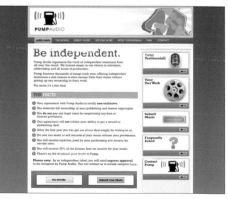

Info DESIGN AND PROGRAMMING: Rob Tourtelot <www.telodesign.com>. /// TOOLS: HTML, PHP, CSS, Macromedia Flash, Adobe Illustrator, Adobe Photoshop, Sorenson Squeeze. /// CONTENTS: Information about Pump's no-fee, non-exclusive licensing to television, advertising, film and web, FastTrack Mp3, video reels; artist testimonials linking to artist sites, etc. /// DOWNLOAD: Pump's License Agreement for independent artists, Pump Audio's independent artist badges linking back to artists' work. /// COST: 240 hours.

REELWORLD

www.reelworld.com

Highlights The site dynamically resizes depending on the amount of content being delivered. Jingles are preloaded one at a time so users can listen to a jingle immediately despite the progress of other jingles in a package. /// Le site se dimensionne dynamiquement en fonction du nombre de contenus fournis. Les jingles étant préchargés un par un, les utilisateurs peuvent choisir d'en écouter un immédiatement, indépendamment de la progression du contenu du progiciel. /// Die Website passt sich dynamisch in der Größe an, je nachdem wieviel Inhalte geliefert werden. Der Besucher kann so wie ein professioneller Radio DJ harmonisch nahtlose Übergänge vom Jingle zum Song hören.

Info DESIGN: Eric Jordan, Jonathan Moore, Baz Pringle (2Advanced Studios) <www.2advanced.com>. /// FLASH PROGRAMMER/FUNCTIONAL ARCHITECT: Brad Jackson (2Advanced Studios). /// TOOLS: Macromedia Flash, Adobe Photoshop, PHP, CMS, mySQL, 3D Studio Max, Cinema 4D, Maya, Adobe After Effects, Sound Forge. /// CONTENTS: audio. /// DOWNLOAD: demo tracks. /// AWARDS: Flash In The Can Design 2006 (Winner), Technology Awards (Audio Category-Winner), Summit Creative Awards 2006 (Gold), OC ADDY Awards 2006 (Merit), Netscape's Cool (Site of the Day), FWA (Site of the Day). /// COST: 200 hours.

RINOCEROSE

FRANCE
2005

www.rinocerose.com

Highlights

Very minimal animation & design, makes use of the cover art, and elements from the album's artwork (Guitar, Amp...), readability. /// Animation et design très minimalistes, en concordance à la couverture, utilisation d'éléments de l'artwork de l'album (guitare, ampli,...), lisibilité. /// Minimale, dem Cover entsprechende Animation und Design. Die Website verwendet Elemente der Album-Illustrationen (Gitarre, Verstärker...). Lesbarkeit.

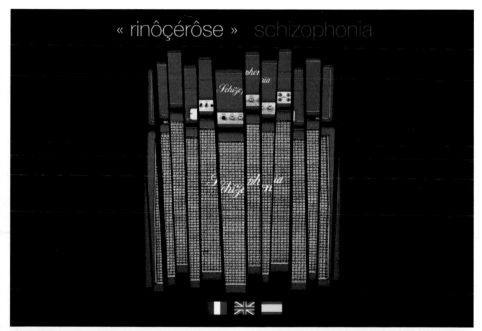

Info

DESIGN AND PROGRAMMING: Emile Shahidi <www.arcademode.com>. /// TOOLS: Adobe Illustrator, Adobe Photoshop, Macromedia Flash, Php, xml. /// CONTENTS: photos, videos, audio songs, album information, discography, playlists. /// DOWNLOAD: pictures. /// COST: 2 weeks.

SOUTH AFRICAN MUSIC AWARDS

SOUTH AFRICA

www.samusicawards.co.za

2006

Highlights

The site combines a proprietary online digital entry submission and judging system; interactive seat booking system; and a public interface which includes a press office, official Nominees album listening post, a full list of nominees, etc. /// Le site allie un système propriétaire d'évaluation et de soumission on-line numérique ; un système interactif de réservation ; et une interface publique comprenant un service de presse, un dispositif d'écoute des nominés officiels, etc. /// Die Website bietet ein geschütztes Online Digitalzugriff-System und ein interaktives Buchungssystem für Platzreservierungen. Über ein öffentliches Interface findet man das Pressebüro, kann in die Alben von offiziellen Kandidaten hineinhören, etc.

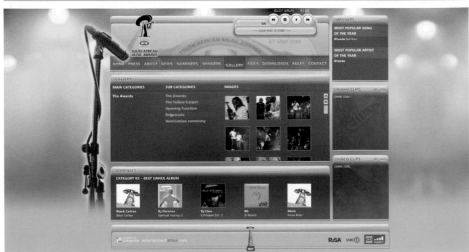

Info

DESIGN AND PROGRAMMING: Prezence SA <www.prezence.co.za>. /// TOOLS: Php, MySql, xHTML, CMS, CSS, Javascript, XML, CMS, Macromedia Flash, Adobe Photoshop, Macromedia Dreamweaver. /// CONTENTS: online digital entry submission, judging system, interactive seat booking system. Public interface (press office, official Nominees album listening post, a full list of nominees, etc). Photo gallery, news, jukebox, audio and video recordings, nominees & winners. /// DOWNLOAD: wallpapers, screensaver, press releases, video and audio recording. /// COST: 100 hours.

Highlights

The world's leading dance event. /// Le plus grand événement dance au monde. /// Der führende Dance-Event der Welt

Yves Deruyter

He started his DJ career about 10 y
ago playing in famous Belgian clubs
as: Globe, Barocci, Cherrymoon, Ill
Extrema, Bel-Air, Carat, Maxx, and
others... Once a month (on Frida
plays in Fuse (B) (Mad Club). As so
DJ's he also started an artist career.
then he is signed to Bonzai Records
first single Animals became a big cl
in Belgium.

At this stage people started wat
artists like Yves Deruyter for playin
big raves (clubs) such as May Day,
Parade, Energy, Nature One, Tr
Energy, Inner City, Mystery land, Gont
Frequance, Inside Out, Passion, Gou-
skitchen, The Gallery, Slinky, Frisky, Gate-
crasher, I love Techno, Axion Beach Rock
Antwerp is Burning, Clubland and so
many more... With his second single h
made a big jump into the German market

Tom Harding

"Tom Harding represents the new so'
of dance music" Mixmag 2005

Tom Harding has been pioneering u
ground dance music on the dance
of Europe for the past ten years. H
won awards from Mixmag, Club UK
Muzik, he quickly found himself pla
into the DJing super league and, b
he knew it, was spinning alongside
legends as Carl Cox, Andy Weatheral
Laurent Garnier at the tender age o
With a high profile start like this
perhaps not surprising that over a de
later Tom is regarded as a leading figl
the international dance music scene
was when Tom headlined the 60,0
strong Dance Valley festival in Hollanc
billed above the likes of Carl Cox, Hard-
floor and Goldie that he truly came of age
Since then he has been the subject o'
BBC, ITV, TMF and MTV documentaries

DESIGN AND PROGRAMMING: thePharmacy <www.thepharmacy-media.com>.))) TOOLS: 3D Studio Max, Adobe Photoshop, Adobe Illustrator, PHP, MySQL,
cromedia Flash. /// CONTENTS: 3D animated navigation, video interviews, streaming video, timelapse video, sound FX & special FX, win tickets game.
WARDS: FWA (Site of the Day) /// COST: 150 hours.

SHARISSA

www.sharissa.com

Highlights

Sharissa's website embodies her luscious sound, juxtaposed with urban style. The site is a true portrait of her spirit and individuality, and helps to form a more personal connection with her audience. /// Le site de Sharissa incarne parfaitement sa sonorité sensuelle, associée à un style urbain. Véritable portrait de son esprit et de sa personnalité, le site l'aide à nouer des rapports plus intimes avec son public. /// Sharissa's Website verkörpert ihren satten Sound, kombiniert mit einem urbanen Stil. Die Site ist ein wahres Portrait ihrer Seele und Individualität und hilft ihr, eine persönlichere Verbindung zu ihrem Publikum zu schaffen.

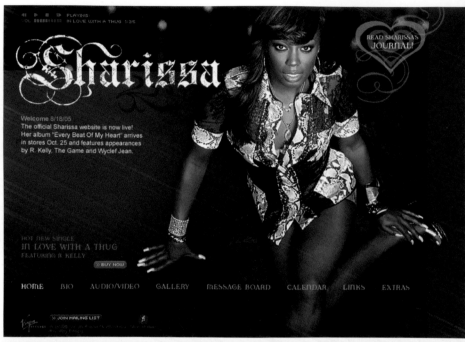

Info

DESIGN AND PROGRAMMING: Fahrenheit Studio <www.fahrenheit.com>. /// TOOLS: Macromedia Flash, Adobe Photoshop, Adobe Illustrator, CMS, HTML. /// CONTENTS: photos, audio/video, tour, bio, journal, animation, message board. /// DOWNLOAD: photos, wallpapers, buddy icons. /// AWARDS: Horizon Interactive Award. /// COST: 100 hours.

SHAYNE WARD

www.shayne-ward.com

Highlights: Striking design highlighting Shayne's creative re launch. Fan image gallery. Fan review uploads. /// Un design choc mettant en valeur la dernière création de Shayne. Galerie photos et téléchargements pour les fans. /// Eindrucksvolles Design, das Shayne's kreative Wiedereinführung hervorhebt. Bildgalerie und Rückblick-Upload für Fans.

DESIGN AND PROGRAMMING: Ten4 Design <www.ten4design.co.uk>. /// TOOLS: CMS, php, Mysql, Adobe Photoshop. /// CONTENTS: photos, audio, music videos, uploads [add reviews/images]. /// DOWNLOAD: mobile [ringtones/phone wallpapers] audio tracks, Mp3, wallpapers, screensavers, photos. /// COST: 2 weeks.

SMS CREW

www.smscrew.com

Highlights

Detailed flash animations integrating small 3D animated sequences. Hidden goodies forcing the Net surfer to reconsider the site and to spend more time on it. /// Des animations Flash très soignées composent de petites séquences en 3D. Toutes sortes de 'plus' invitent l'internaute à parcourir le site et à y passer davantage de temps. /// Detaillierte Flash-Animationen integrieren kleine 3D animierte Abläufe. Versteckte Leckerbissen zwingen den Websurfer, die Website wieder aufzurufen und mehr Zeit auf der Site zu verbringen.

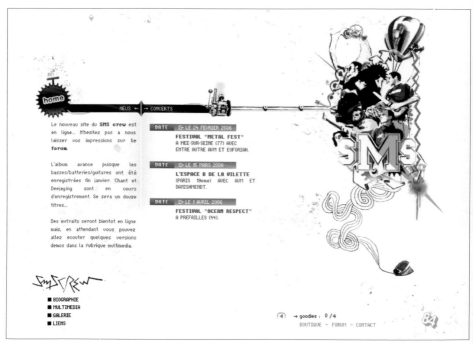

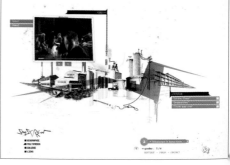

Info

DESIGN AND PROGRAMMING: Olivier Bienaimé [Les 84] <www.les84.com>. /// **TOOLS:** Adobe Photoshop, 3D Studio Max, Adobe After Effects, Macromedia Flash, PHP, XML. /// **CONTENTS:** photo, video-clips, extracts of song, hidden-goodies (wallpapers, samples, word of track), animations. /// **DOWNLOAD:** Mp3, wallpapers, word of track, pressbook and roadbook. /// **AWARDS:** FWA (Site of the Day), Fcukstar, Pixelmakers, Styleawards, featured on ventila ca, pixelsurgeon.com, uailab.com, lookom.com. /// **COST:** 60 hours.

SOHODOLLS

www.sohodolls.co.uk

Interactive street scene, streaming MP3 player, interactive voodoo doll that you can pin to your heart's content. /// Scène de rue interactive, lecteur streaming MP3, poupée vaudou interactive sur laquelle il faut cliquer pour accéder à ses contenus favoris. /// Interaktive Straßenszene, MP3-Player Streaming, interaktive Voodoo-Puppe, in die man so viele Nadeln stechen kann wie man will.

Info DESIGN: Matt Rice, Hege Aaby, Rosie Bryant (Sennep) <www.sennep.com>. /// PROGRAMMING: Matt Rice, Julien Fournier (Sennep). /// TOOLS: Adobe Photoshop, Macromedia Flash, Macromedia Freehand, Sorenson squeeze, Adobe After Effects, Adobe Illustrator, PHP, MySQL, XML. /// CONTENTS: gig listings, Mp3 player, latest news, videos, galleries, biography, forum, links. /// DOWNLOAD: Free promotional tracks. /// COST: 6 weeks.

SONY BMG RECORDS

www.sonybmgmusic.co.uk

Highlights

Completely redesigning and restructuring of the UK arm of this international music behemoth. /// Le blason britannique de ce Léviathan de la musique internationale, entièrement repensé et restructuré. /// Komplett verändertes Design und neue Struktur des UK-Zweiges dieses internationalen Musikgiganten.

Info

DESIGN AND PROGRAMMING: Kleber Design Ltd. <www.kleber.net>. /// TOOLS: Adobe Photoshop, Macromedia Flash, php, HTML, CMS. /// CONTENTS: label news, artist biographies, releases, audio and video previews. /// COST: 4 weeks.

STUPEFLIP
www.stupeflip.com

Highlights

Dynamic content. Back office. /// Contenus dynamiques. Suivi des commandes. /// Dynamischer Inhalt. Back office.

Info

DESIGN: Stephane Bellenger <www.qaqaprnduq.com>. /// PROGRAMMING: Fabrice Depoix <www.clebar.com>. /// TOOLS: Macromedia Flash, PHP, XML, CSS.
/// CONTENTS: video, photo, animations, sounds. /// COST: 100 hours.

Highlights

Big site, very short turnaround. /// Grand site, se renouvelle sans cesse. /// Große Website, sehr schnelle Updates.

Info

DESIGN: Rose Pietrovito (dZinenmOtion) <www.dzinenmotion.com>. /// **TOOLS:** Adobe Photoshop, Macromedia Flash. /// **DOWNLOAD:** Mp3. /// **AWARDS:** FWA.

SUSAN GRAY

www.susangray.com

Highlights

Susan Gray's site is an all Flash website with the text content drawn in via XML. The site features rich textures and beautiful imagery. The transitions from section to section are smooth and tasteful. /// Le site de Susan Gray est entièrement en Flash, avec des textes conçus en XML. Riches textures des fonctions et beauté des images. Entre section et section, les transitions sont souples et agréables. /// Susan Gray's Site ist eine komplette Flash-Website, bei dem die Textinhalte über XML geschrieben wurden. Die Site bietet satte Texturen und schönes Bildmaterial. Die Übergänge von Ausschnitt zu Ausschnitt verlaufen weich und geschmackvoll.

Info

DESIGN AND PROGRAMMING: driftlab <www.driftlab.com>. /// **TOOLS:** Adobe Photoshop, Macromedia Flash, XML, PHP. /// **CONTENTS:** photos, tour dates, news, events, biographical sketch, song samples. /// **AWARDS:** FWA. /// **COST:** 40 hours.

SVINKELS
www.svinkels.com

Highlights Strong design identity with subtle animations. /// Design à très forte personnalité et animations subtiles. /// Starke Design-Identität mit raffinierten Animationen.

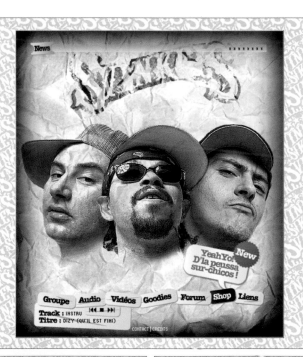

Info DESIGN: Nicolas "Mook" Alanquand <www.qhuit.com>. /// PROGRAMMING: Emile Shahidi <www.arcademode.com>. /// TOOLS: Adobe Illustrator, Adobe Photoshop, Macromedia Flash, Php, xml. /// CONTENTS: photos, videos, audio songs, lyrics, album information, discography. /// DOWNLOAD: wallpapers, screensavers. /// COST: 1 month.

TEDDY GEIGER
www.teddygeigermusic.com

USA

2006

Highlights

A navigation that makes you stay on the site, with great music playing on the fly. A great example to escape from the normal "window" navigation while maintaining a great design and information accessibility. /// Système de navigation qui vous colle à votre siège, et musique à la volée. Un bel exemple pour qui souhaite échapper à la "fenêtre" de navigation normale sans sacrifier ni le design, ni l'accessibilité. /// Die Site bietet eine Navigation, die den Websurfer auf der Website hält und läßt dabei im Hintergrund großartige Musik laufen. Ein phantastisches Beispiel dafür, wie auf die normale "Window"-Navigation verzichtet werden kann, mit hervorragendem Design und Informationszugang.

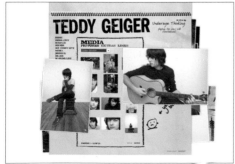

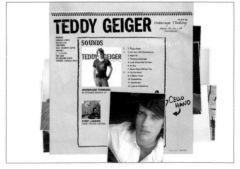

Info

DESIGN AND PROGRAMMING: Sparkart LLC. /// TOOLS: Adobe Photoshop, Macromedia Flash, In-house CMS. /// CONTENTS: news, photos, videos, discography, tours, biography, blog, tabs. /// COST: 1 month.

THE KOOKS

www.thekooks.co.uk

Highlights

The Kooks cheeky faces and great songs! /// Les bouilles insolentes des Kooks, et de grandes chansons ! /// Die Website bietet die frechen Gesichter von The Kooks und ihre großartigen Songs!

Info

DESIGN AND PROGRAMMING: Smiling Wolf <www.smilingwolf.co.uk>. /// TOOLS: Macromedia Flash, Macromedia Dreamweaver, HTML, XML, CMS, Adobe Photoshop, Adobe Illustrator, Canon EOS300D, pens, pencils, masking tape, etc. /// CONTENTS: photos, video-clips, sound files, tour dates, special features, competitions, etc. /// DOWNLOAD: tracks, videos, screensavers, lyrics. /// AWARDS: Roses Advertising Award 2006.

THE LODGE

www.thelodge.com/musicproduction

Highlights

The site includes many of Flash 8's new features, XML data for all content, plus some PHP code behind the scenes. /// Le site inclut plusieurs nouvelles fonctions en Flash 8, des données XML pour tous les contenus, plus quelques codes PHP derrière les scènes. /// Die Website integriert viele der neuen Funktionen von Flash 8, XML-Daten für die Inhalte und einige PHP-Codes für die Szenen.

Info

DESIGN: Kevin Cavallaro (Tanka Design) <www.tankadesign.com>. /// PROGRAMMING: Jeff Falcon. /// TOOLS: Adobe Photoshop, Adobe Illustrator, Macromedia Flash, On2 Flix Pro, PHP, XML. /// CONTENTS: photography, video, music, 4-track music mixer, file transfer. /// COST: 5 weeks.

Highlights

The guitarist's hat! /// Le chapeau du guitariste ! /// Der Hut des Gitarristen!

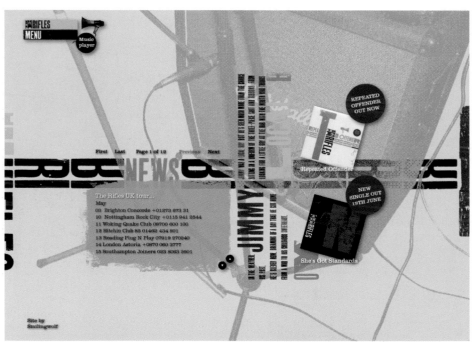

Info

DESIGN AND PROGRAMMING: Smiling Wolf <www.smilingwolf.co.uk>. /// **TOOLS:** Macromedia Flash, CMS, XML, Adobe Photoshop, Adobe Illustrator, Quicktime Pro, Sony Mini DV DCR HC90E, letterpress(!). /// **CONTENTS:** photo, video-clips, tour, animation.

Highlights

As an information medium, a great example of how to have a good mixture of digital and analogue strategy. /// En tant que media d'information, un bel exemple de mélange réussi entre stratégie numérique et analogique. /// Als ein Informationsmedium stellt die Website ein großartiges Beispiel dafür dar, wie eine gute Mischung aus digitalen und analogen Strategien aussieht.

Info

DESIGN AND PROGRAMMING: Rootylicious & plotDesign Group.US <www.rootylicious.com>. /// TOOLS: Macromedia Studio, Adobe Studio, CMS, php. /// CONTENTS: magazine features, video clips, audio player. /// DOWNLOAD: ringtones, Mp3 singles. /// COST: 2 months.

TNGRM

www.tngrm.com

Highlights

TNGRM is the collaborated site with the music maker Yoshiteru Himuro. electronic music and sound blog. Fresh interaction. /// TNGRM est un site en collaboration avec le compositeur Yoshiteru Himuro. Musique électronique et blog sonore. Brillamment interactif. /// TNGRM ist eine Website in Zusammenarbeit mit dem Musikproduzenten Yoshiteru Himuro. Elektronische Musik und Sound-Blog. Tolle Interaktion.

himuro released new album.
mild fantasy violence *from zod records US*

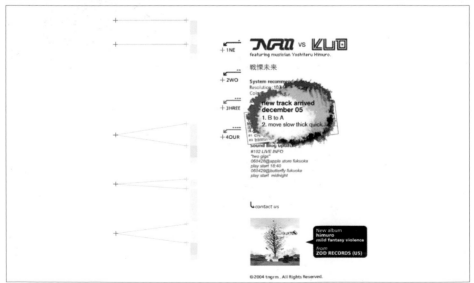

Info

DESIGN: Keigo Anan & Yoshiteru Himuro <http://photo.tngrm.com>. /// PROGRAMMING: Keigo Anan. /// TOOLS: Adobe Photoshop, Adobe Illustrator, Macromedia Flash, CMS, PHP and right hand (for clicking the mouse). /// CONTENTS: tracks, sound blog, Flash interaction. /// DOWNLOAD: Mp3. /// COST: 30 days.

TRIO KATHARSIS

ROMANIA
2006

www.triokatharsis.com

Highlights

Video intensive sections, global audio player and track visualization mixed with content music. /// Sections vidéo intenses, lecteur audio global et piste visuelle mixée avec contenu musical. /// Viele Videoausschnitte, globaler Audio-Player und Titel-Visualisierung gemischt mit Musikinhalten.

Info

DESIGN: Vlad Ardeleanu <www.raise-media.com>. /// PROGRAMMING: Zoltan Csibi <www.raise-media.com>. /// TOOLS: php, Adobe Photoshop, Macromedia Flash, Adobe After Effects. /// CONTENTS: photo, video-clips, Mp3 tracks. /// COST: 100 hours.

THE TROUBADOUR

www.troubadour.com

Highlights

A new History section features a timeline of the venue's milestones and key events. Month-to-month calendar view of all events and act details leads to a clear ticket purchase process. /// Une nouvelle fonction Historique comprend une éphéméride des prochains événements marquants du local. L'agenda 'mois par mois' détaillé des spectacles conduit à une fonction très pratique permettant d'acheter ses places. /// Der neue Geschichtsbereich bietet eine Zeitleiste über die Meilensteine und wichtigsten Events der Veranstaltung sowie eine Diashow. Die monatliche Kalender-Ansicht zu allen Events und Spieldetails führt zu einem übersichtlichen Ticket-Bestellbereich.

Info

DESIGN: Ed Lu (Cottonblend) <www.cottonblend.com>. /// PROGRAMMING: Ismail Elshareef (Cottonblend). /// ACCOUNT MANAGER: Julie Woo. /// TOOLS: Adobe Photoshop, Adobe Illustrator, Macromedia Flash, Macromedia Fireworks, Custom Database-Driven CMS, PHP/MySQL, XHTML, FreeBSD, Macromedia Dreamweaver. /// CONTENTS: event calendar, history, ticketing and FAQ, photos, map. /// DOWNLOAD: Specifications (floor-plan, lighting, stage layout, technical rider). Fax form (for easy purchases). /// COST: 220 hours.

Highlights

For a production company, a website like this is the perfect example of how you can create impact on customers whoever they are. /// *Pour une société de production, un tel site Web montre parfaitement comment faire impression sur le consommateur, quel qu'il soit.* /// Für eine Produktionsfirma ist eine Website wie diese ein perfektes Beispiel dafür, wie man auf Kunden Einfluss nehmen kann, wann auch immer sie online sind.

Info

DESIGN: Rose Pietrovito (dZinenmOtion) <www.dzinenmotion.com>. /// TOOLS: Adobe Photoshop, Macromedia Flash. /// CONTENTS: Video and Mp3 clips.

VIVA.TV

www.viva.tv

GERMANY

2006

Highlights Many prelistenings per week, daily fresh news and gossip, exclusive content, by now more than 2000 full length music videoclips! /// Chaque semaine, beaucoup de choses à écouter en avant-première, et chaque jour des nouvelles et des indiscrétions, des contenus exclusifs et plus de 2000 vidéoclips longue durée jusqu'ici ! /// **Viele Vorschauen pro Woche, täglich aktuelle Nachrichten und Klatsch, exklusive Inhalte und jetzt mehr als 2000 Musik-Videoclips in ganzer Länge!**

Info DESIGN: gosub communications gmbh <www.gosub.de>. /// PROGRAMMING: exozet interact <www.exozet.com>. /// TOOLS: XHTML, CSS2, Exozet CMS R4, PHP, MySQL, Adobe Photoshop, Eclipse, Macromedia Flash. /// CONTENTS: starbased stories, news, charts, video-clips, photo-galleries, prelistenings, tours, raffles, style (fashion & beauty), webradio, tickets, merch. /// DOWNLOAD: prelistenings, photos. /// COST: 5 months.

WARP RECORDS

www.warprecords.com

UK
2001

Highlights

A site of its time. /// Un site de son temps. /// Eine Website ihrer Zeit.

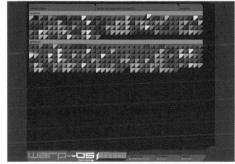

Info

DESIGN: The Designers Republic <www.thedesignersrepublic.com>. /// **PROGRAMMING:** Kleber Design Ltd. <www.kleber.net>. /// **TOOLS:** Adobe Photoshop, Macromedia Flash, php, HTML, CMS. /// **CONTENTS:** label news, artist biographies, releases, shop, audio and video previews. /// **AWARDS:** Net Excellence, Prix Ars Electronica 2001 / (Best Independent Label Site) NME net sounds 2001 / Best Website, Musik und Machine 2001. /// **COST:** 6 months.

WARREN SUICIDE

www.warrensuicide.com

Highlights

It's flash but with a chainsaw. The crazy characters of warrens courtyard. Capturing the bands off beat sense of humour. /// Du Flash à la tronçonneuse. Les personnages déjantés de warrens courtyard. Tout à fait dans le ton de l'humour noir du groupe. /// Flash mit der Kettensäge. Die verrückten Figuren von Warren's Hinterhof. Fängt den ungewöhnlichen Sinn für Humor der Band ein.

Info

DESIGN: Tim Dillon (Onscreen Creative) <www.onscreencreative.com>. /// PROGRAMMING: Rob Thomson, Zulma Patarroyo <www.marotori.com>. /// ILLUSTRATIONS: "Cherie" (band member). /// TOOLS: Pen and Paper, Adobe Photoshop, Adobe Illustrator, Macromedia Flash, PHP CMS. /// CONTENTS: music studio, chat room, gallery, band bio, shop links, members area with secret login and downloads. /// DOWNLOAD: PDF cut out warren mask, Mp3 samples, wallpapers. /// COST: 7 weeks.

WATERSHED

www.watershed.co.za

Having scooped the coveted Internet Tiny Award for excellence in web design and development skills, watershed.co.za offers you the chance to buy official merchandise to show your support for local talent. /// Lauréat du Tiny Award aux meilleurs design et talent créatif, prix Internet parmi les plus convoités, watershed.co.za vous offre l'opportunité d'acheter des produits officiels pour manifester votre soutien aux talents locaux. /// Nachdem watershed.co.za den begehrten Internet Tiny Award für hervorragendes Webdesign und Entwicklung eingeheimst hat, wird dem Fan die Möglichkeit geboten, offizielle Fanartikel über die Site zu erwerben, um seine Unterstützung für lokale Talente zu zeigen.

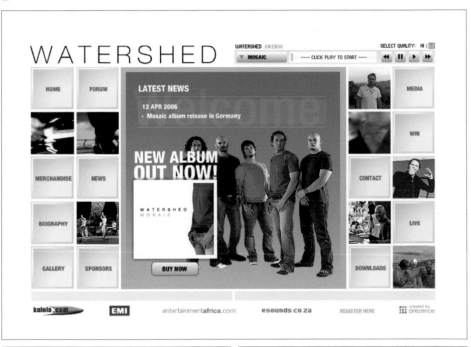

Info

DESIGN AND PROGRAMMING: Prezence SA <www.prezence.co.za>. /// TOOLS: Php, MySql, xHTML, CMS, CSS, Javascript, XML, CMS, Adobe Photoshop, Macromedia Flash, Macromedia Dreamweaver. /// CONTENTS: photo gallery, media (video), wallpapers, jukebox (all albums), tour dates, news, competitions. /// DOWNLOAD: wallpapers. /// AWARDS: TINY. /// COST: 50 hours.

WILL YOUNG

www.willyoung.co.uk

Highlights Exclusive video content for the site. Interactive footage. Fan image gallery and fan review uploads. /// Contenus vidéo exclusifs pour le site. Métrage interactif. Galerie photos et revue à télécharger pour les fans. /// Exklusiver Video-Inhalt für die Website. Interaktives Filmmaterial. Fan Bildgallerie und Rückblick-Download.

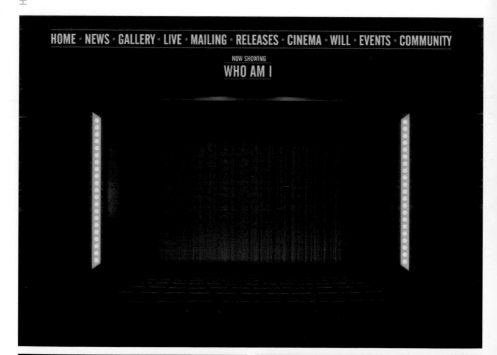

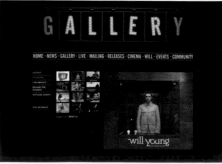

Info DESIGN AND PROGRAMMING: Ten4 Design <www.ten4design.co.uk>. /// TOOLS: CMS, php, MySql, Macromedia Flash, Adobe Photoshop. /// CONTENTS: photos, interactive Flash video, animation, games, audio, uploads (add reviews/images). /// DOWNLOAD: samples, audio tracks, Mp3, wallpapers, screensavers, photos, podcasts. /// COST: 1 month.

WIPEOUT PURE

UK
2005

Highlights

First Flash based remixer application. Ability to synch and download remixed tracks to PSP device. /// Première application de remix en Flash. Permet de synchroniser et de télécharger des morceaux remixés sur PSP. /// Erste Flash-basierte Remix-Anwendung. Synchronisations- und Download-Möglichkeit von Remix-Titeln auf PSP.

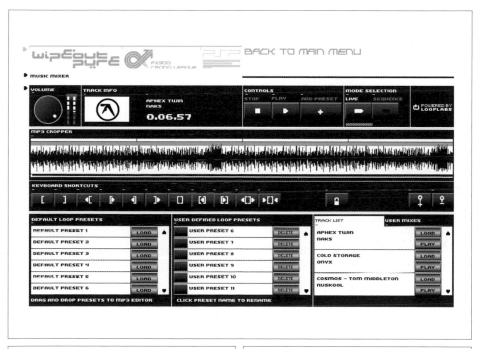

Info

DESIGN: CRASH!MEDIA <www.crashmedia.com>, Bubble Media <www.bubblemedia.co.uk>. /// PROGRAMMING: CRASH!MEDIA <www.crashmedia.com>. /// TOOLS: Adobe Photoshop, Macromedia Flash. /// CONTENTS: Mp3 tracks. /// DOWNLOAD: ability to download remixed tracks to PSP. /// COST: 400 hours.

MUSIC SITES · 185

ZEN FESTIVAL

www.zenfestival.com

Highlights

Check out video and audio clips from musicians featured in Zen Festival events. Stunning graphics created by Shane Mielke (2Advanced Studios). /// Consultez des vidéos et des audio clips de musiciens à l'affiche du Zen Festival. Stupéfiantes images graphiques dues à Shane Mielke (2Advanced Studios). /// Der Besucher findet Video- und Audioclips von Musikern, die bei Zen Festival-Events vorgestellt wurden. Hervorragende Graphik von Shane Mielke (2Advanced Studios).

Info

DESIGN: Shane Mielke, Ken Donnellan, Mark Wisniowski (2Advanced Strudios) <www.2advanced.com>. /// **PROGRAMMING:** Shane Mielke, Ken Donnellan (2Advanced Studios). /// **TOOLS:** PHP, CMS, XML, Adobe Photoshop, Adobe After Effects, Macromedia Flash. /// **CONTENTS:** photo, video, audio. /// **COST:** 2 weeks.

ZERO 7

Highlights

Creative animation approach combining after effects and flash. Flexible layouts can be turned on and off by the band. Exclusive site only tracks can be played through jukebox. /// Animation extrêmement créative associée à des effets et à du Flash. Mise en page flexible pouvant être mise en / hors service par le groupe. Morceaux à écouter sur juke-box à balayage aléatoire. /// Kreativer Animationsansatz, der Effekte und Flash kombiniert. Die flexiblen Layouts können von der Band an- und ausgeschaltet werden. Exklusive Titel können über eine Jukebox gespielt werden.

Info

DESIGN: Tim Dillon (Onscreen Creative) <www.onscreencreative.com>, Dave Stansbie (The Creative Corporation) <www.thecreativecorporation.co.uk>. /// PROGRAMMING: Rob Thomson <www.marotori.com>. /// TOOLS: Adobe Photoshop, Adobe Illustrator, Macromedia Flash, PHP CMS. /// CONTENTS: animated intro, jukebox, video player, news, tour dates, discography, shop links and lots of music. /// COST: 4 weeks.

BRYAN INGRAM

www.24-7media.de/ingram

USA

2004

Highlights

The site has an overall retro/Jules Verne type of style and an audio player. It is one of the most daily ripped layouts we have done so far. /// Allure complètement rétro, façon Jules Verne, et aspect de radio collector. L'une des mises en page les plus épatantes que nous ayons réalisées jusqu'ici. /// Der gesamte Retro/Jules Verne-Stil und der Audio-Player. Eines des am häufigsten gerippten Layouts, das wir bisher gemacht haben.

Info

DESIGN AND PROGRAMMING: 247 Media Studios <www.24-7media.de>. /// TOOLS: Adobe Photoshop, Adobe After Effects, Macromedia Flash. /// CONTENTS: music, photos, text. /// AWARDS: FWA, ADA. /// COST: 3 weeks.

5FM MUSIC

www.5fm.co.za

SOUTH AFRICA

2006

Highlights

Aside from stunning new visuals and greater functionality, the new 5FM website centres on more lifestyle-related content & ties in on- and off-air content by increasing interactivity between DJs and listeners. /// À part de stupéfiants nouveaux visuels et davantage de fonctionnalité, le nouveau Web de 5FM est axé sur un contenu plus quotidien, et associe les contenus sur et hors antenne en augmentant l'interactivité entre DJ's et audience. /// Neben verblüffenden neuen Ansichten und größerer Funktionalität zentriert sich die neue 5FM Website auf mehr Lifestyle-Inhalte und verbindet Radioinhalte und Website-Inhalte durch eine Steigerung der Interaktivität zwischen DJs und Hörern.

Info

DESIGN AND PROGRAMMING: STONEWALL+ <www.stonewall.co.za>. /// TOOLS: XHTML, CSS, Macromedia Flash, ASP.NET. /// CONTENTS: lifestyle content, news, music, movies, podcasts, blogs, image galleries and mobile content. /// DOWNLOAD: podcasts, movies, wallpapers and mobile content. /// COST: 3 months.

I would like to thank first of all Daniel Castelo (as he named himself artistically), or just Daniel, my assistant in the whole series that has not just worked in all designs and layouts, but as a musician and composer has a great ability with the subject of this book. Making these guides has been a challenge to surprise and to give something of value in every edition we do. This is a guide to use now and later as a testimony to what we all have gone through. Daniel Siciliano Brêtas (now the real complete name) has a great understanding as both maker and consumer of these guides.

I have to thank all studios and professionals participating in the book again, for their contribution and effort to provide the materials and information that enriched this book. They are the labels, the artists, the brilliant designers featured here, the managers, the recording companies, and anyone that has helped somehow.

Moreover, Stefan Klatte, our brilliant prepress man, for guiding us always in the technical details and helping us making a better job every day.

One special thanks go also to the four contributors that have taken time to show the different points of views of how the web touches everyone's life, in this case from a music perspective. The Brazilian artist Ed. Motta, the manager of Sony-BMG in the UK Daniel Ayers, Craig Swann from Crashmedia and finally Jonathan Sulkow, the designer of the new Madonna.com website. You must read the text and pay attention to what they say. Hope you will discover lot's of new things when reading the publication. Have a nice journey (with a soundtrack this time)!

Julius Wiedemann

IMPRINT

Web Design: Music Sites

To stay informed about upcoming TASCHEN titles,
please request our magazine at
www.taschen.com/magazine or write to TASCHEN,
Hohenzollernring 53, D-50672 Cologne, Germany,
contact@taschen.com, Fax: +49-221-254919.
We will be happy to send you a free copy of our
magazine which is filled with information about all
of our books.

Design & Layout: Daniel Siciliano Brêtas
Production: Stefan Klatte

Editor: Julius Wiedemann
Assitant-editor: Daniel Siciliano Brêtas
French Translation: Martine Joulia
German Translation: Daniela Thoma
Spanish Translation: María del Mar Portillo
Italian Translation: Marco Barberi
Portuguese Translation: Alcides Murtinheira

Printed in Italy
ISBN-13 978-3-8228-4958-3
ISBN-10 3-8228-4958-8

TASCHEN is not responsible when web addresses
cannot be reached if they are offline or can be
viewed just with plug-ins.

Web Design: E-Commerce
Ed. Julius Wiedemann /
Flexi-cover, 192 pp. / € 6.99 /
$ 9.99 / £ 4.99 / ¥ 1.500

Web Design: Flash Sites
Ed. Julius Wiedemann /
Flexi-cover, 192 pp. / € 6.99 /
$ 9.99 / £ 4.99 / ¥ 1.500

Web Design: Portfolios
Ed. Julius Wiedemann /
Flexi-cover, 192 pp. / € 6.99 /
$ 9.99 / £ 4.99 / ¥ 1.500

"These books are beautiful objects, well-designed and lucid." —*Le Monde*, Paris, on the ICONS series

"Buy them all and add some pleasure to your life."

African Style
Ed. Angelika Taschen

Alchemy & Mysticism
Alexander Roob

All-American Ads 40ˢ
Ed. Jim Heimann

All-American Ads 50ˢ
Ed. Jim Heimann

All-American Ads 60ˢ
Ed. Jim Heimann

American Indian
Dr. Sonja Schierle

Angels
Gilles Néret

Architecture Now!
Ed. Philip Jodidio

Art Now
Eds. Burkhard Riemschneider,
Uta Grosenick

Atget's Paris
Ed. Hans Christian Adam

Berlin Style
Ed. Angelika Taschen

Cars of the 50s
Ed. Jim Heimann, Tony
Thacker

Cars of the 60s
Ed. Jim Heimann, Tony
Thacker

Cars of the 70s
Ed. Jim Heimann, Tony
Thacker

Chairs
Charlotte & Peter Fiell

Christmas
Ed. Jim Heimann, Steven Heller

Classic Rock Covers
Ed. Michael Ochs

Design Handbook
Charlotte & Peter Fiell

Design of the 20ᵗʰ Century
Charlotte & Peter Fiell

Design for the 21ˢᵗ Century
Charlotte & Peter Fiell

Devils
Gilles Néret

Digital Beauties
Ed. Julius Wiedemann

Robert Doisneau
Ed. Jean-Claude Gautrand

East German Design
Ralf Ulrich / Photos: Ernst Hedler

Egypt Style
Ed. Angelika Taschen

Encyclopaedia Anatomica
Ed. Museo La Specola
Florence

M.C. Escher

Fashion
Ed. The Kyoto Costume
Institute

Fashion Now!
Ed. Terry Jones, Susie Rushton

Fruit
Ed. George Brookshaw,
Uta Pellgrü-Gagel

HR Giger
HR Giger

Grand Tour
Harry Seidler

Graphic Design
Eds. Charlotte & Peter Fiell

Greece Style
Ed. Angelika Taschen

Halloween
Ed. Jim Heimann, Steven
Heller

Havana Style
Ed. Angelika Taschen

Homo Art
Gilles Néret

Hot Rods
Ed. Coco Shinomiya, Tony
Thacker

Hula
Ed. Jim Heimann

Indian Style
Ed. Angelika Taschen

India Bazaar
Samantha Harrison, Bari Kumar

Industrial Design
Charlotte & Peter Fiell

Japanese Beauties
Ed. Alex Gross

Krazy Kids' Food
Eds. Steve Roden,
Dan Goodsell

Las Vegas
Ed. Jim Heimann,
W. R. Wilkerson III

London Style
Ed. Angelika Taschen

Mexicana
Ed. Jim Heimann

Mexico Style
Ed. Angelika Taschen

Morocco Style
Ed. Angelika Taschen

New York Style
Ed. Angelika Taschen

Paris Style
Ed. Angelika Taschen

Penguin
Frans Lanting

20ᵗʰ Century Photography
Museum Ludwig Cologne

Photo Icons I
Hans-Michael Koetzle

Photo Icons II
Hans-Michael Koetzle

Pierre et Gilles
Eric Troncy

Provence Style
Ed. Angelika Taschen

Robots & Spaceships
Ed. Teruhisa Kitahara

Safari Style
Ed. Angelika Taschen

Seaside Style
Ed. Angelika Taschen

Albertus Seba. Butterflies
Irmgard Müsch

**Albertus Seba. Shells &
Corals**
Irmgard Müsch

Signs
Ed. Julius Wiedeman

South African Style
Ed. Angelika Taschen

Starck
Philippe Starck

Surfing
Ed. Jim Heimann

Sweden Style
Ed. Angelika Taschen

Sydney Style
Ed. Angelika Taschen

Tattoos
Ed. Henk Schiffmacher

Tiffany
Jacob Baal-Teshuva

Tiki Style
Sven Kirsten

Tuscany Style
Ed. Angelika Taschen

Valentines
Ed. Jim Heimann,
Steven Heller

Web Design: Best Studios
Ed. Julius Wiedemann

Web Design: Flash Sites
Ed. Julius Wiedemann

Web Design: Portfolios
Ed. Julius Wiedemann

**Women Artists
in the 20ᵗʰ and 21ˢᵗ Century**
Ed. Uta Grosenick